POLICE USE OF FORCE:
OFFICAL REPORTS,
CITIZEN COMPLAINTS,
AND
LEGAL CONSEQUENCES

BY:

ANTONY M. PATE AND

LORIE A. FRIDELL

WITH THE ASSISTANCE OF

EDWIN E. HAMILTON

POLICE FOUNDATION

The Police Foundation is a public, nonprofit research and technical assistance group established by The Ford Foundation in 1970 and dedicated to improving policing in America. The research findings in this publication were supported under award number 91-IJ-CX-0028 from the National Institute of Justice, Office of Justice Programs, U.S. Department of Justice. Points of view in this document do not necessarily represent the official position of the U.S. Department of Justice.

ISBN 1-884614-01-9 (Volume 1)
ISBN 1-884614-00-0 (2 Volume Set)

Library of Congress Catalog Card Number: 93-86909

ACKNOWLEDGEMENTS

This report is the result of the prodigious efforts of far more people than we can possibly name here. To all of those people, regardless of whether we were able to mention them personally, our most profound acknowledgements and thanks.

The funding for the research reported here was provided by the National Institute of Justice, whose director at the time, Charles B. (Chuck) DeWitt, recognized the need to learn more about the critical topic of the use of force by police. Michael Russell, his successor, has steadfastly supported us throughout this endeavor.

Our project monitor at the National Institute of Justice, Dr. Craig Uchida, has offered encouragement and advice from beginning to end.

Dr. Brian Reaves, at the Bureau of Justice Statistics, provided advice (and, of course, statistics) whenever called upon.

At the Police Foundation, our particular thanks go to Sampson Annan, who oversaw the massive work of conducting the national survey, and to Virginia Burke, who worked so diligently to bring the pieces together. To Earl Hamilton, we owe a special debt. Without his arduous data analysis work, this project would not have been possible.

We owe particular gratitude to the International Association of Chiefs of Police, who assisted us in developing and pre-testing the questionnaire used in this project and in encouraging law enforcement agencies to respond to it.

Our work has been strengthened by the constructive advice offered by the six anonymous scholars and practitioners retained by the National Institute of Justice to review the first draft of this report. Although we cannot thank them by name, our appreciation is indicated by the changes we have made in response to their helpful comments.

Last, but by no means least, we express our gratitude to the 1,111 law enforcement agencies that took the time to complete the rather time-consuming questionnaire upon which this study is based. We sought to make this work worthy of your support.

We extend credit and acknowledgements to all of those people who contributed to this project. We alone are responsible for any errors or oversights.

Antony M. Pate   Lorie A. Fridell

FOREWORD

In the best of all worlds, there would be no need for police. In that world, there would be no conflict and people would obey the law. For as long as history has been recorded, however, it has been clear that society requires formal mechanisms to maintain order and enforce compliance with the law. Relatively recently, society has turned to our police to provide that formal mechanism.

In the second best possible world, compliance with our police would be voluntary. As a former police officer and chief executive of one of America's largest police departments, I can attest to what history has shown—that police officers must use force in order to do their job effectively. Indeed, the legitimate use of force is the defining characteristic of the institution of policing.

The provision of such power to the police, however, has always been a double edged sword. Long before Lord Acton warned that power corrupts, and absolute power corrupts absolutely, the Romans were asking *"Sed quis custodiet ipsos custodes?"*, or "Who will guard the guards themselves?"

This concern about the use of force by law enforcement officers was reflected in the articles of the Magna Carta, imposed by the English barons on King John in 1215. Reflecting a desire to prevent police abuse of power, false arrest, oppression, and contempt of the law, that compact is replete with restrictions upon the police of those days, the sheriffs, bailiffs, and constables. And the remedies of that ancient time were similar in many ways to those proposed today: recruit better police officers, stiffen the penalties for malfeasance, and create a civilian review board as an external control upon the police.

The ambivalent attitude about police in general, and their use of force in particular, has endured. This ambivalence, for example, was reflected in the intense political debates waged, first in the United Kingdom, and later in the United States, concerning the creation of modern police departments. As historians relate those debates, public fear about the possible abuses of power by an organized police agency was overcome only by the greater fear of riots and crime that occurred in the early nineteenth century. Police, then, were begrudgingly created as an institutional "counter-force" against the broader forces of disorder.

In 1829, Sir Robert Peel succeeded in establishing a full-time day and night patrol force in London, under the control of two commissioners appointed by the home secretary. Even after the first of these officers began to walk the streets in their distinctive blue uniforms, the ambivalence about their use of force, including the types of force available to them, was evident. Although the police in Ireland had been carrying firearms since the 1780's, it was considered prudent to arm the English "bobbies" only with truncheons. Even these weapons, however, had to be kept concealed in the tail pockets of their uniform coats, to be drawn only in self-defense. Unnecessary clubbing, it was feared, would threaten the moral basis of police authority and arouse public antagonism. Only in 1863 were officers allowed to wear their truncheons exposed, and even then they were to be kept in a leather case suspended from the belt.

Compliance to the policy of use of truncheons was, at first, left largely to the discretion of individual officers, under the occasional supervision of their supervisors. As soon as 1830, however, a spate of complaints of police violence led the commissioners to issue a strict policy stipulating that the truncheon was not to be used in response to insulting language or actions that did not endanger the police officer, and threatening severe disciplinary action or dismissal for violation of these restrictions. This initiative seemed to work, as indicated by a decline in citizen complaints.

Reflecting a trend found throughout the history of policing, the attitudes toward and policies concerning the use of force by police reflected the level of social turmoil. During the Chartist tensions of 1842 and the "great scare" of 1848, for instance, some constables were armed at night with cutlasses. Any officer, however, who drew his sword on duty had to report the circumstances to his sergeant and to the desk officer when he returned to the station house. Again, the use of the sword was to be only for defensive purposes, with termination threatened if it were even drawn for less serious causes. As soon as these crises abated, however, the swords were removed, leaving the officers armed once again only with truncheons.

When the new form of policing was introduced in the United States, the institution took on uniquely American characteristics. First, instead of being accountable to the national government, the American police, with the exception of a few federal agencies, were under the control of municipal, county, and state governments. As a result, policing in America became the most decentralized in the world, spread across almost 16,000 jurisdictions, reflecting a myriad of different structures, policies, and procedures. Thus, instead of having one method of defining and controlling the use of force, there were thousands.

The second major difference between American policing and that found in England was the society in which such policing operated. As a nation born in armed revolution and preserved by a bloody civil war, the United States displayed a dramatically higher level of violence than its mother country. Since most American police departments were formed a few years after Samuel Colt patented his revolver in 1835, this violence soon took the form of armed attacks on the officers themselves. In response, individual officers took it upon themselves to purchase and carry firearms, often with the unofficial support of their supervisors. An ambivalence toward the use of force similar to that demonstrated in England was evident in the United States. The police commissioner in New York City, for example, acquiesced in the use of revolvers by his officers, but did not officially authorize it or admit that weapons were purchased for the officers' use (even though officers were provided with cardboard holsters with the department's name on them) until it became impossible to deny it.

The ambivalence regarding the use of force resulted in a lack of clear guidance, in the form of training and policies, provided to officers. As a result of this lack of specific departmental guidance, police were often left to make their own decisions concerning what force to use and when to use it. The individual attitudes of peers and supervisors about the use of force came to play a prominent role in affecting those decisions.

Particularly problematic was the determination of the amount of force that was "necessary" to make an arrest. Making arrests in the early years of policing was a particularly onerous task. Arresting officers not only had to face a generally disrespectful public but, because most arrests were for drunkenness and public disorder, arrestees frequently resisted and officers had to physically subdue them. Once a suspect was subdued, the officer faced the problem of transporting the suspect, on foot, back to the station house.

During the course of the 20th century, increasing public attention has been paid to the use of force by police, often concentrating on those occasions when it was used, or alleged to be used, unnecessarily or to excess. A series of official inquiries probed the issue. The Wickersham Commission in 1931 devoted one of its reports, *Lawlessness in Law Enforcement*, to the problem of brutality and the third degree.

In the last quarter of a century, courts, legislatures, and law enforcement officials themselves have provided clearer guidance concerning the use of force by police. In particular, the United States Supreme Court has provided guidance concerning the legal constraints involved in the use of force, particularly when making arrests or apprehending fleeing felons. In addition, the courts have generally imposed responsibility upon municipalities for the torts of their police officers, causing those financially stretched governments to pay more attention than ever to the use of force by those officers. State legislatures have enacted laws delimiting the appropriate use of force by police officers. Law enforcement agencies have instituted more restrictive policies and procedures to limit the use of force by their personnel.

In the last decade, the job of the police officer has, if anything, become even more difficult than ever before. The widespread presence of firearms, including semi-automatic and automatic weapons, coupled with gang activity, drug trafficking, and rampant disregard for human life, has made the daily routine of police a matter of life and death. Efforts to provide police with methods and weapons, including less than lethal devices such as the Taser and Mace of various types, have intensified.

Despite attempts to control it, the perception of the use of excessive force by police contributed to the Harlem disturbance of 1935, the Watts riot in 1965, the wide range of 1967 disorders studied by the Kerner Commission, the Miami riot of 1980, and several other disturbances. The Police Foundation itself was created in 1970 largely as a result of the need, made undeniably clear by the riots of the 1960s, to understand and improve the functioning of America's police, including the controlled application of the use of force.

The destruction and death resulting from the reaction to the acquittal of the officers accused of beating Rodney King in 1991 created a situation in which it became no longer possible to look with ambivalence upon the use of force by police. Recognizing that the use of legitimate force is crucial to effective policing, but that there was a critical need for baseline information about the extent to which such force is currently used and the consequences of that use, the Police Foundation, with support from the National Institute of Justice, conducted a comprehensive national survey of law enforcement agencies to provide such information. This report presents the results of that survey in the expectation that, armed with these findings, jurists, legislators, scholars, and law enforcement executives can make informed public policy decisions that will effectively address the issue of police use of force.

Hubert Williams
President
Police Foundation

ABSTRACT

The legitimate use of force is the defining feature of the role of police in society. In fact, the police must be allowed to use force when necessary to achieve lawful police objectives. Unfortunately, however, the public is usually made aware of police use of force only on those occasions when the use of force is, or appears to be, excessive.

Despite the critical importance of the use of force in policing, little is known about the extent or nature of that use, the methods by which agencies monitor force, how often citizens complain that excessive force was applied, what happens to those complaints, how frequently allegations of excessive force result in lawsuits, and how those suits are resolved.

Recognizing the need for further research on these issues, the National Institute of Justice provided support to the Police Foundation to conduct a comprehensive national survey of law enforcement agencies to address these questions.

A total of 1,111 law enforcement agencies completed an extensive questionnaire designed to address issues pertaining to the important topic of police use of force.

This report presents a review of existing literature on the use of force by police, describes the methods by which the survey was conducted, presents the results of the key issues addressed by the survey, and discusses the research and policy implications of the results.

Table of Contents

LIST OF FIGURES

LIST OF TABLES

I. INTRODUCTION

Egon Bittner, in his pioneering classic *The Functions of Police in Modern Society*, argues convincingly that:

> ...the capacity to use coercive force lends thematic unity to all police activity in the same sense in which...the capacity to cure illness lends unity to everything that is ordinarily done in the field of medical practice (1970:42).

In more concrete terms, he went on to contend (1970: 43) that:

> ...the role of the police is to address all sorts of human problems when and insofar as their solutions do or may possibly require the use of force at the point of their occurrence. This lends homogeneity to such diverse procedures as catching a criminal, driving the mayor to the airport, evicting a drunken person from a bar, directing traffic, crowd control, taking care of lost children, administering medical first aid, and separating fighting relatives.

In the Bittner tradition, many subsequent scholars have found it useful in defining the role and function of police to argue that the legitimate use of coercive force is the critical factor distinguishing policing from all other professions and distinguishes police officers from all other citizens. Sherman (1980: 2), for example, stated, "The essence of government is a monopoly on the nonpunishable use of force, and modern governments delegate that monopoly to police officers."

More recently, Klockers (1985: 9-10) concluded:

> No police anywhere has ever existed, nor is it possible to conceive of a genuine police ever existing, that does not claim a right to compel other people forcibly to do something. If it did not claim such a right, it would not be a police.

Seen in this light, it is reasonable to expect that our police would use force as an everyday part of their job. Indeed, the police *must* be allowed to use force when necessary to achieve legitimate police objectives. Without this capacity, they would be unable to function effectively.

However, as pointed out by Kerstetter (1985: 149), it is precisely because "the *appropriate* use of coercive force" defines modern police, that "the inappropriate use of coercive force is the central problem of contemporary police misconduct." Any use of force by police must be constrained by the laws that they are bound to uphold. Any violation of those laws can be expected to undermine the public support and credibility that the police need to function effectively. As shown by the recent riots in Los Angeles, the loss of trust in police, and the resulting diminution in their effectiveness, can have far-reaching consequences. The societal consequences of police excessive use of force, however, predate the destruction and death in Los Angeles and throughout the nation. One need only refer to history books to recall that the Chicago riot of 1919, the Harlem disturbance of 1935, the Watts riot of 1965, the wide range of disorders in 1967, the Miami riot of 1980, and many other similar episodes stemmed in large part from public perceptions of police misconduct and excessive force.

Despite the vital importance of the use of force by police, little is currently known about the use of force by law enforcement officers, department policies regarding the reporting of such force, the extent to which force is alleged to be used excessively, what types of officers and citizens are involved in incidents of alleged excessive force, and how law enforcement agencies respond to allegations of excessive force.

Recognizing the need for further understanding of these issues, the Police Foundation received funding from the National Institute of Justice to conduct a comprehensive study of police use of force involving a national survey of law enforcement agencies. The responses to that survey provide the first national data on the extent to which law enforcement officers use force, the types of force used, the force reporting requirements of law enforcement agencies, the procedures for receiving and processing complaints of excessive force, the numbers and rates of civilian complaints of excessive force received, the dispositions of those allegations, and the frequency and dispositions of lawsuits alleging the use of excessive force.

The remainder of this report identifies what is known—and not known— about the use of force by police, describes how the national survey was conducted, and presents a summary of the most pertinent findings of that survey and discusses the research and policy implications of the results.

II. POLICE USE OF FORCE: WHAT IS KNOWN, WHAT NEEDS TO BE LEARNED

In this chapter we review the current state of knowledge about police use of force generally, and the use of excessive force, in particular. In the first part of this chapter, we discuss the various categories of force. After that, we describe the limited information available concerning the extent to which police use force in general and excessive force in particular. We also review what is known about the relationship between departmental policies, procedures, and practices and (1) the levels and characteristics of incidents involving the use of force and use of excessive force, and (2) the levels of excessive force complaints and the dispositions of these complaints.

As will be seen by this review of the literature, despite the importance of these issues, relatively little is known about the extent to which police use force, the types of force used, the extent to which force results in citizen complaints, the procedures for processing those complaints, and the extent to which those complaints are determined by the departments to be justified. The results from the survey, described in Chapter IV, provide the first national data on these topics.

A. TYPES OF FORCE

"Force" is "the exertion of power to compel or restrain the behavior of others" (Kania and Mackey, 1977:29). Police force can be classified as "non-deadly" or "deadly," "violent" or "non-violent," and "reasonable" or "excessive." Force is "deadly" if it is likely to cause death or serious bodily harm, and, thus, "non-deadly" if it is *not* likely to cause death or serious bodily harm. Deadly force is always violent (that is, physical); non-deadly force can be physical or non-physical. Non-physical force would include officer presence and verbal commands (see e.g., Clede, 1987).

Figure 1 provides a "Use of Force Scale," indicating the force options available to officers. The options range from verbalization through non-deadly force to use of deadly force. Both "justifiable force" and "excessive force" can cut across any of these levels. Most of the literature has focused on force that is physical (that is, violent). Legally, excessive force by police is that amount of *physical* force that is more than *reasonably necessary* to effect a legal police function. Consistent with this, Kania and Mackey (1977:29) acknowledge that police violence can be both "proper and improper" and define "excessive force" as "violence of a degree that is more than necessary or justified to effect a legitimate police function."

FIGURE 1

Use of Force Scale

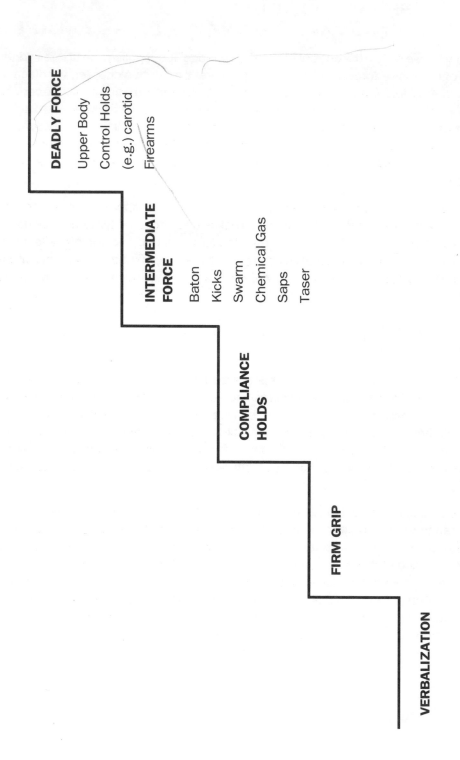

DEADLY FORCE

Upper Body
Control Holds
(e.g.) carotid

Firearms

INTERMEDIATE FORCE

Baton
Kicks
Swarm
Chemical Gas
Saps
Taser

COMPLIANCE HOLDS

FIRM GRIP

VERBALIZATION

SOURCE: Independent Commission of the Los Angeles Police Department (1991)

A broader definition would encompass excessive force that is non-violent, as well. This broader conceptualization is portrayed in the Use of Force Model in Figure 2. This model implies a very broad definition of "excessive force" by including the non-physical police conduct. It specifies the proper use of force by an officer for various categories of opponent/subject action. According to Desmedt (1984:172), "the subject's threat/resistance level determines the necessary amount of force the officer uses." Using less force than is necessary in light of subject action is termed "ineffective control." Using too much force is "excessive control."

Fyfe (1987) expands the concepts further by distinguishing between two types of lawful violence in an untraditional way: "necessary violence" and "unnecessary violence." "Unnecessary violence," he explains, "occurs when well-meaning officers lack the skills to resolve problems with as little violence as possible, and, instead, resort to force that might otherwise have been avoided" (Fyfe, 1987:6). This type of violence is lawful (per his categorization), but avoidable.

Even these definitions and figures do not remove the ambiguity from the concept for officers, departments, and researchers. Because it is not possible to articulate the specific appropriate force responses of officers for every conceivable situation, the "reasonably necessary" standard as judged by the "reasonable person" is required. However, this leaves officers to find that narrow line, portrayed on Figure 2, that "wobbles between proper practice and excessive violence" (Manning, 1980:140). A typical department policy directs officers to use amount and type of force that is reasonable and necessary under the circumstances.

One focus of the national survey conducted by the Police Foundation was departmental policies and practices pertaining to physical force—both deadly and less than lethal—used by law enforcement officers.

B.   INCIDENCE AND PREVALENCE OF FORCE

There is little information available regarding the extent to which police use force, even deadly force. This is due, in large part, to the difficulty of obtaining data. The study of police use of force began with a focus on deadly force. Within that area, the official data first available were city-level frequencies of firearms homicides by police officers. Later, data on firearms hits (deaths and woundings) became available, and subsequently, data on shots fired. These data became increasingly available as cities started to keep track of these types of incidents for internal purposes. Today, virtually all departments maintain this information. (See Alpert and Fridell, 1992, for a discussion of the advances over time within the study of deadly force.)

A much more recent phenomenon is the adoption of "use of force" forms by some departments in which officers report information for each incident in which either deadly or less than lethal force is used. Few studies on force have relied on use of force forms and, instead, have relied on observational or survey data. Below we describe the limited amount of information available which pertains to the incidence and prevalence of police use of force, including excessive force.

figure 2

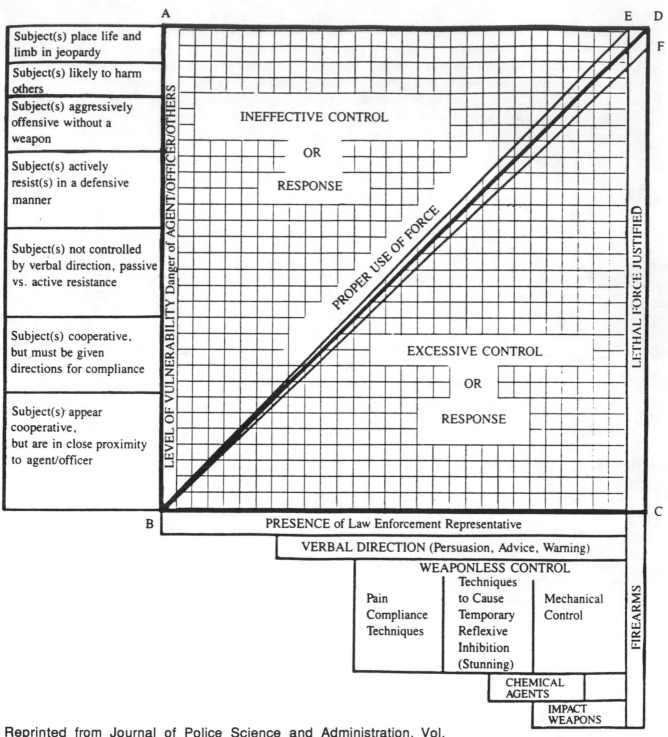

Reprinted from Journal of Police Science and Administration, Vol. 12, No. 2, page 173, 1984. Copyright held by the International Association of Chiefs of Police, 515 N. Washington Street, Alexandria, VA 22314, USA. Further reproduction without express written permission from IACP is strictly prohibited.

Reiss (1968), Friedrich (1980), Bayley and Garofalo (1989), and Worden (1992) report that the use of force by police is infrequent. Black and Reiss (1967) collected information on 3,826 police-citizen encounters in three cities during the summer of 1966. Using these data, Reiss (1971, and later Friedrich, 1980, using the same data) determined that force was used in 5.1 percent of the 1,565 incidents "in which the police came into contact with citizens they regarded as at least potential offenders" (Friedrich, 1980:86). In the small proportion of incidents in which force was used, the force was determined to be reasonable in 65 percent of those incidents and excessive in 35 percent.

 Lundstrom and Mullan (1987) measured the amount of force used by the St. Paul Police Department between March 1, 1985, and February 28, 1986 (a 12-month period). Specifically, the research focused on custody situations: both those involving arrests and those involving the transport of individuals to detoxification centers and/or mental hospitals. Of 11,989 custody situations, 1,750, or 14.6 percent, involved officer use of force. The custody situations most likely to lead to force were those involving disorderly conduct, petty assault, and aggravated assault. Those situations involved force in 54.2, 30.5, and 21.5 percent of incidents, respectively. The researchers did not attempt to distinguish between reasonable and excessive force.

Worden (1992) conducted secondary analyses on data collected in 1977 for the Police Services Study. Trained observers collected data on 5,688 police-citizen encounters during 900 patrol shifts in 24 police departments in three metropolitan areas. He found that police used force in just 60 of the 5,688 (1.05%) police-citizen encounters. In one-third of those encounters where force was used, the observer adjudged the force to be excessive or unnecessary. Among those encounters that involved suspects (as opposed to citizens who were not suspects), reasonable force was used in 2.3 percent of the encounters and improper force was used in 1.3 percent. The remaining 96.4 percent of the incidents involving suspects did not involve force.

Various studies have surveyed citizens to determine whether they have been the subject of police misconduct, have seen police misconduct, or heard about police misconduct. It is important to note that these studies relied on the subjects' interpretations of what defined "misconduct." A survey conducted for the National Advisory Commission on Civil Disorders (Campbell and Schuman, 1969) asked citizens in 15 cities about their negative experiences with police. Seven percent of the blacks and 2 percent of the whites claimed that police had "roughed them up."

Bayley and Mendelsohn (1969) surveyed 806 citizens in Denver, Colorado, in 1966 about, among other things, their experiences and their friends' and neighbors' experiences with "police brutality." Claiming to have personally experienced police brutality were 4 percent of the Caucasians, 9 percent of the blacks, and 15 percent of the persons with Spanish surnames. A full 30 percent of the blacks reported that they had heard of charges of police brutality from their friends and/or neighbors, compared to 4 percent of the Caucasians and 12 percent of the persons with Spanish surnames.

A survey of citizens within a representative sample of U.S. cities found that 13.6 percent of the respondents believed that they had been victims of some sort of police misconduct during the previous year (Whitaker, 1982). Only one-third of the persons who claimed to have been mistreated filed a formal complaint with the police.

Another source of information regarding the extent of police use of excessive force is surveys of law enforcement personnel. For instance, in the same study described above, Bayley and Mendelsohn surveyed 100 officers of the Denver Police Department. These researchers report (1969) that 53 percent of the officers acknowledged that they had witnessed an "incident that *someone* might consider to constitute police brutality" (p. 128, emphasis added). Twenty-seven percent of the officers maintained that they witnessed incidents that, in their opinion, involved "harassment or the excessive use of force" (p. 129).

Barker (1978, reprinted in 1991) surveyed 43 officers in a small southern city, asking them to estimate what percent of their fellow officers engaged in specified deviant activities. In addition to police brutality (defined as "excessive force on a prisoner"), Baker asked about police perjury, sex on duty, drinking on duty, and sleeping on duty. On the average, officers reported that 40 percent (39.19%) of their fellow officers have used excessive force on a prisoner. This was perceived as equally prevalent as sleeping on duty (an average of 39.58 percent) and more prevalent than any of the other deviant activities.

A major reason why we know so little about the extent to which police use force, and the extent to which this force is used excessively, is that the measurement of these phenomena is so difficult. None of the measures used in the studies described above to assess incidence and prevalence of force is without validity problems. Observational studies are unlikely to generate sufficient data for generalizing and suffer from the probable reactivity of the officers to being the subject of observation. Citizen surveys or interviews measure perceptions of force or excessive force that may differ considerably from legal definitions. Surveys or interviews with police also reflect perceptions and may solicit socially desirable responses.

Data collected from agency records have drawbacks, as well. First of all, official data from any government agency reflects the agency perspective and may or may not fully represent reality. Relatedly, researchers who have studied force within individual departments, most likely achieved access to the most progressive departments, which were more amenable to scrutiny. Another problem is that information from departmental records on force are frequently incomplete and variations across departments may be so great that it could be inappropriate to assume that the data from an individual department, or several departments, is representative of law enforcement in the United States. In terms of excessive force, departments can only provide data on complaints of excessive force and/or sustained complaints of excessive force, both of which are only indirect measures, at best, of actual behavior.

One of the purposes of the current survey was to determine the extent to which departments keep records on the use of force. Additionally, the survey collected from those agencies that keep these types of records data regarding the extent to which officers use force. These data have never before been collected on so large a scale. They allow for the first time, for some general conclusions to be made regarding the use of force by U.S. law enforcement. Chapter IV presents the information regarding the extent to which departments mandate that officers report the use of various types of force and the rate at which each type of force was reported to have been used per 1,000 sworn officers in 1991. These data are presented for four types of agencies: sheriffs' departments, county police departments, city police departments, and state law enforcement agencies. Finally, within each agency type, the results are presented by agency size.

In the following section we review the research that has attempted to determine the effects of departmental policies, procedures, and practices on the use of force.

C. DEPARTMENTAL POLICIES, PROCEDURES, AND PRACTICES AND THE USE OF FORCE

Some research has addressed the effects that law enforcement policies, procedures, and practices have had on the use of and response to both the reasonable and excessive use of force. Important in this line of inquiry are policies, procedures, and practices directly related to the use of force and the departmental response thereto, as well as policies, procedures, and practices related to recruitment and selection, assignment, supervision, promotion, and so forth. Research on departments has also focused on training and its impact on the use of force.

C.1 POLICY RESTRICTIVENESS AND THE USE OF FORCE

Some research at the departmental level has focused specifically on the effect of policy restrictiveness and policy enforcement on police use of force. For instance, Uelman (1973) conducted one of the earliest studies on deadly force policy. He collected information from 50 police agencies in Los Angeles County to assess policy content, effectiveness, and enforcement. He found great diversity across jurisdictions in terms of policies regarding the use of deadly force against fleeing felons, and found, as one would expect, that shooting rates correlated with policy restrictiveness. He found that the departments in the most restrictive policy category had approximately one-half the shooting rates of departments with the least restrictive policies. The shooting of fleeing felons accounted for a large part of the differences in rates, which corresponded with the differences in policies. However, this researcher found departments with more restrictive policies had fewer defense of life shootings, as well.

Fyfe (1978) documented the effects of a new shooting policy and new shooting review procedures in New York City. The New York City Police Department adopted a more restrictive policy in 1972, which delimited further a Forcible Felony statute and provided for a Firearms Discharge Review Board to investigate and evaluate all discharges by department police. Fyfe studied all police discharges in that city between January 1, 1971, and December 31, 1975, to assess the effect of this more restrictive shooting policy and the more comprehensive follow-up procedures on the "frequency, nature, and consequences of police shooting in New York City" (p. 312). He found a "considerable reduction" in police firearms discharges following the policy modifications. The greatest reduction was in the "most controversial shootings," that is, those involving fleeing felons or the prevention or termination of a crime. Similarly, Meyer (1980) found a reduction in police shootings following the implementation of a more restrictive policy in Los Angeles, and Sherman (1983) reported reductions in police gun use in Atlanta, Georgia, and Kansas City, Missouri, following policy changes. Most of the studies that documented decreases in shooting rates following implementation of more restrictive policies also found no increase in risk of harm to officers (Fyfe, 1978; Sherman, 1983).

C.2 POLICY ENFORCEMENT AND USE OF FORCE

Persons researching force policies have emphasized that the *content* of the guidelines is not the only departmental factor related to use of force rates. Skolnick and Fyfe (1993) described events at several cities wherein the content of restrictive written shooting policies was overwhelmed by the much more lax unwritten policies of the top administrators. Similarly, Sherman (1983) maintained that findings of reduced shootings following policy adoption in the cities he looked at (123):

> do not suggest that these results can be achieved by the mere invocation of a written policy. The policy changes in each of these cities were all accompanied by intense public criticism of the police and an increasingly severe administrative and disciplinary posture toward shooting.

Other researchers, too, have documented the effects of "administrative posture regarding compliance" (Waegel, 1984:137) and, relatedly, enforcement modes. So, for instance, Fyfe noted the importance, not only of the new, more restrictive shooting policy in New York City, but also the establishment of the Firearms Discharge Review Board for policy enforcement. Waegel (1984) examined police shootings in Philadelphia between 1970 and 1978 to assess department compliance with a statutory change in deadly force law that occurred in 1973. The change was from a common law any-fleeing-felon law to a forcible felony statute. Waegel found "substantial noncompliance" with the new law. He reported that 20 percent of the shooting incidents after the statute change were unlawful, suggesting that "statutory change alone may not be sufficient to bring about desired changes in police behavior" (p. 136). Instead, he argued that without an administrative stance that the law will be complied with, the changes in behavior called for by a statutory revision will not occur.

Uchida (1982) evaluated the implementation process and outcome of "Operation Rollout" in Los Angeles in the late 1970s. This intervention changed the way in which police-involved shootings were investigated. Specifically, Operation Rollout involved the Los Angeles District Attorney's Office in the on-scene, as well as follow-up, investigations of all officer-involved shootings. It was hypothesized that a more "full, fair, objective, independent, and timely" review process would reduce the frequency of police shootings (p. 189). Uchida's data indicated that officer-involved shootings decreased following the adoption of Operation Rollout, though he cautioned that "it cannot be said with certainty how much of that change was a result of Rollout" (p. 272).

The findings of the Independent Commission on the Los Angeles Police Department confirms other findings of research in deadly force, that policies and procedures are insufficient in the absence of an administrative posture demanding compliance. This is reflected in the statement by the Independent Commission (1991:32): "The problem of excessive force in the LAPD is fundamentally a problem of supervision, management, and leadership." This was also a theme in the recent American Civil Liberties Union release on "Police Brutality and its Remedies" (1991). This report maintained that the way in which officers in the field carry out the police mission is "heavily influenced by the leadership of their department" (1991:6). Particular emphasis was placed upon the role of the chief of police in setting the tone within the department (p. 6):

> When incidents of brutality, misconduct or racism occur, the chief's immediate reaction to these incidents will have a great impact on whether the incident will be repeated in the future.

The tone can be conveyed by the detection and punishment of misconduct, but more positively, by reinforcing appropriate conduct. Toch (1969:243) argued that "if an officer recruits citizens to his side in a conflict situation, or befriends someone who approaches him belligerently, or disarms a man without force, his effectiveness deserves commendation." Additionally, examples such as these of defusing violence should be used as "positive training materials." Manning (1980:144), too, advocated changing the formal and informal reward structure to reinforce the defusing of violence.

One aspect of policy enforcement is departmental use of force reporting requirements. An increasing number of departments are requiring officers to submit reports for each incident in which force is used. As indicated above, the national survey determined the extent of this adoption and these results are contained in Chapter IV. Also relevant to policy enforcement is the extent to which complaints of policy violations are scrutinized and violations are punished. This issue is discussed in a later section and was incorporated in the national survey.

C.3 RECRUITMENT/SELECTION

One intervention to reduce the use of unnecessary or excessive force by police is to screen, at the hiring stage, persons particularly inclined toward violence. A major problem, however, is developing screening devices that are valid measures of this propensity. Some research has attempted to determine what, if any, individual characteristics of officers are linked to the use of force, and particularly to the use of excessive force. Toch (1969, 1984) claimed that there exist violence-prone people who "invite violence-prone interactions" (1984:225). Similarly, the Independent Commission on the LAPD (1991) determined that a large proportion of excessive force incidents are concentrated among a small number of officers. Studies have looked at demographic variables, attitudes, work-related factors, and other characteristics of officers to determine whether differences exist between officers who use force and officers who do not. More scarce, yet much more pertinent, is research identifying characteristics that differentiate officers who do and do not use excessive force.

C.3.1 OFFICER CHARACTERISTICS AND THE USE OF FORCE

Walker (1982) looked at the relationship between officer characteristics and "attitudes toward violence" ("the attitudes of a subject toward accepting violence as a way of solving problems" p. 95). He found no statistically significant differences in attitudes between males and females, but found statistically significant positive correlations between acceptance of violence and a childhood history of physical punishment and involvement in sports. Further, younger subjects had more positive attitudes toward violence than older subjects.

In her study of use of force forms submitted to the Rochester, New York, police department between 1973 and 1979, Croft (1985) compared officers who used force frequently with officers who did not, controlling for duty assignment and arrest exposure. Paralleling the findings regarding use of deadly force, Croft found that officers who used more force were significantly younger. Relatedly, these persons had fewer years of service and were younger when appointed to the department. Also assessing the effects of age, Cohen and Chaiken (1972) found that older officers had fewer complaints filed against them, including complaints of excessive force. Friedrich (1980:89) reported that "there is only the slightest indication that more experienced officers use force more reasonably and less excessively than less experienced officers."

Cohen and Chaiken (1972) found that more educated officers had fewer citizen complaints. Similarly, Cascio (1977) found that more educated officers had fewer allegations against them of excessive force. In contrast, Croft (1985) found no differences between the high- and low-use-of-force officers in terms of their educational level. Similarly, she found no differences between the two groups with regard to prior military service, civil service test ranking, height, number of days lost from work due to sickness or injury, public and departmental evaluation (including number of citizen complaints, sustained citizen complaints, civil charges, internally-initiated complaints, disciplinary charges, or sustained disciplinary charges) and whether the officers were "proactive" or "reactive."

Friedrich (1980) found few characteristics that differentiated officers who used justifiable force and those who used excessive force. However, he reported differences for the variable race (see also Reiss, 1971). He reports that black officers were more likely to use reasonable force, but less likely to use excessive force. The finding regarding greater use of reasonable force is consistent with findings in the deadly force literature (e.g., Geller and Karales, 1981; Fyfe, 1981a). These findings have been attributed to the assignment of black officers to the higher crime areas and to the great propensity for black officers to live in the higher crime neighborhoods (see e.g., Geller and Karales, 1981; Fyfe, 1981a).

Worden (1992) looked at the correspondence between various officer characteristics and the use of reasonable force as well as the use of improper force. Overall, he found that officer characteristics contributed little to explanations of the use of either type of force. Interesting, however, were his findings that black officers, as well as officers who have earned bachelor's degrees, were more likely to use force, but less likely to use improper force. Further, officers were more likely to use force if they "conceive[d] their role in narrow terms" (e.g., believed that the police should not "handle cases involving public nuisances, such as barking dogs or burning rubbish" p. 26), displayed negative attitudes toward citizens, and/or believed that the use of force should be regulated internally by the police.

Of 650 LAPD officers surveyed by the Independent Commission on the LAPD, one-quarter believed that "racial bias (prejudice) on the part of officers toward minority citizens currently exists and contributes to a negative interaction between police and the community." Over one-quarter agreed that "an officer's prejudice towards the suspect's race may lead to the use of excessive force" (1991:69).

Black and Reiss (1967) and Friedrich (1980), came to different conclusions regarding the role of racial prejudice in officers' use of force against blacks, though they used the same source of data. The officers' attitudes toward blacks were assessed based on the conversations between the observers and officers during their lengthy interactions. Reiss (1971) reported that, though more than 75 percent of the officers made prejudiced statements about blacks during the period of observation, the police did not unnecessarily assault black persons or treat black persons "uncivilly" more often than they did whites. Friedrich (1980) claimed that although the differences across prejudiced and non-prejudiced officers were small, "the more prejudiced the police are, the more likely they are to use force against black offenders" (p. 90).

C.3.2 EMPLOYMENT SCREENING DEVICES

The New York State Commission reviewed studies that attempted to assess the relationship between employment screening devices and procedures and the use of excessive force and reported (1987:306):

> Early identification and screening of applicants that are or may be violence prone are ... problematic. In order to develop methods to do so, it is necessary ... to isolate those personality characteristics that are predictive of violent behavior.

The New York Commission suggested additional research to develop screening devices that could be used to identify violence prone persons and additionally, suggested that, since past behavior is the best predictor of future behavior, that background investigations be especially vigorous.

Similarly, the Independent Commission on the LAPD concluded that psychological screening devices "cannot test for ... subtle abnormalities which may make an individual ill-suited to be a police officer, such as poor impulse control and the proclivity toward violence" (p. 110) and also noted that these or related problems might develop after a person joins the force. The Independent Commission noted, as did the New York Commission, the importance of assessing violent histories of applicants. The members expressed dismay at the great attention during background investigations paid to drug use and sexual orientation compared to violent tendencies. The report stated (1991:11):

according to the Personnel Department, the investigators often ask intensely personal and pointed follow-up questions regarding sexual history and use of drugs, while not pursuing a candidate's responses to the questions on violence. As a result, the investigators may not effectively screen out individuals with violent tendencies.

The Commission recommended that increased emphasis be paid to past behavior and less to test and interview results during employment screening and that officers be retested periodically during employment to detect psychological problems.

Addressing issues related to recruitment and selection, the national survey collected data on various characteristics of the sworn personnel in each department. Using these data, in Chapter IV, we compare the characteristics of the officers against whom one or more complaints were filed during 1991 and the characteristics of officers against whom complaints were sustained with the characteristics of officers in general. Further, we present information regarding whether departments require psychological or psychiatric evaluations of their department applicants. These results are presented for various agency types and sizes.

C.4 TRAINING

The Community Relations Service of the U.S. Department of Justice (1989:173) maintains that "training can have a significant impact on all aspects of police service delivery and is of critical importance in the control of police-community violence." Training in the area of deadly force has improved significantly in recent years (see Alpert and Fridell, 1992) and much of that progress has ramifications for the area of less-than-lethal force, as well. Particularly noteworthy are efforts to teach not just *how* to shoot but *when* to shoot. The corresponding application for non-deadly force would be training, not just on less-than-lethal tactics and weapons, but on appropriate utilization. Similarly, programs that have application for less-than-lethal as well as deadly force use would be training in crisis intervention skills, general communication, and social skills, and cultural sensitivity.

The Los Angeles Commission looked at academy training, field training, and in-service training and determined that "in each phase of training additional emphasis is needed on the use of verbal skills rather than physical force to control potentially volatile situations and on the development of human relationship skills to better serve Los Angeles' increasingly diverse population" (1991:121).

Two such specialized training programs geared toward the reduction of unnecessary violence which have been implemented and evaluated are the Metro-Dade Violence Reduction Project of the Police Foundation and the Oakland intervention of Toch, Grant, and Galvin.

"Survival City" of the Metro-Dade Police Firearm Range uses role-playing of police-citizen encounters to "enhance patrol officers' skills in defusing the potentially violent situations they encounter every day" (Fyfe, 1987:1). Officers in groups are assigned various roles, such as that of a perpetrator, bystander, or officer. Fyfe, who with the Police Foundation designed and evaluated the training regimen, emphasized the importance, not just of safety tactics, but of officer sensitivity and politeness when dealing with citizens in order to avoid escalation to violence. In this vein, Scharf and Binder (1983) described the relevance of teaching officers interpersonal skills and crisis intervention skills that may help to defuse confrontations with agitated citizens. Geller (1982) also noted the importance of multi-cultural awareness on the part of officers. He explained (1982:172) that we need to "sensitize officers to ... cultural differences among racial and ethnic groups that might lead officers to misread the dangerousness of a situation on the street."

Toch, Grant, and Galvin (1975) implemented the Oakland project designed to reduce the amount of violence in police-citizen contacts. Instead of designing and imposing the intervention upon the officers, this team turned the tasks of design and implementation over to well-respected officers in the department who had experience with violent confrontations with citizens.

The officers generated various policies and interventions designed to reduce police-citizen violence including an in-service training program for violence-prone officers, a redesign of academy and field training, the development of a Family Crisis Intervention Unit, and the development of an Officer Review Panel.

As pertains to training and the use of force, the national survey collected information from departments regarding the amount of training provided to recruits, the use of Field Training Officer programs, the length of new officer probation, and certain aspects of in-service training. These results are contained in Chapter IV. The results provide comparisons across agency type, size, and geographic location.

C.5 MONITORING AND EARLY WARNING

Since the early 1970's, law enforcement agencies have been using various methods by which to monitor their officers, with a particular interest in detecting officers who are prone to misuse force (FBI, 1991). Information contained within personnel files can be used as part of an "early warning" system designed to help identify violence-prone officers. The United States Commission on Civil Rights (1981:81) pointed out that "the careful maintenance of records is essential to making possible the recognition of officers who are frequently the subject of complaints or who demonstrate identifiable patterns of inappropriate behavior." They described the information maintained by several departments which had developed early warning systems. This information included:

The number of times an officer is assaulted or resisted in the course of making an arrest, as well as the number of injuries sustained by an officer or citizen in confrontations between the two.

The number and outcome of citizen complaints lodged against an officer, alleging abusive behavior or unwarranted use of force. Many such complaints are groundless, and many that would be well-founded are never made; nevertheless, the accumulation of a large number of complaints against an officer may reveal something about that officer's style of policing.

The number of shootings or [firearms] discharges involving an officer.

The picture of the officer presented in supervisory evaluations, interdepartmental memoranda, letters, and other reports.

The New York State Commission (1987) acknowledged the difficulty in pinpointing indicators of an officer who is misusing force, but advocated the development of early warning systems, nonetheless. They reported that 19 of the 30 New York agencies that responded to a survey indicated that they had some form of early intervention system in place.

In Salt Lake City, a policy was implemented whereby officer performance was "inspected" periodically by the department. This involved an inspector interviewing persons with whom the officer had recently interacted—including suspects, witnesses, victims, and so forth. If the inspector came across negative comments, s/he interviewed at least five more citizens. Officers were informed of the outcome of the inspection and given constructive feedback regarding positive and negative points. If "serious problems" were found, in-person counseling would result. Reportedly, one year after implementation of the program, complaints against police had dropped from five per day to an average of five per month (Smith, 1974).

The Bakersfield Police Department initiated in 1967 a program whereby officers tape recorded all officer-citizen contacts. The program was developed as a result of citizen complaints of officer discourtesy. Following implementation of this monitoring program, complaints of discourtesy dropped to near zero (Broadaway, 1974).

Related to the monitoring of force, the national survey collected information on whether departments systematically review use of force reports and whether and how departments intervene with officers identified as using unnecessary or excessive force.

C.6 CONCLUSION

In this section we have described research that links departmental policies, practices, and procedures to the use of reasonable or excessive force by police. A major drawback to the research in this area is the focus on a single jurisdiction or, at best, several jurisdictions within studies. Additionally, a vast majority of the studies have focused on municipal police departments, neglecting sheriffs' departments, county police departments, and state agencies. Because of this narrow focus, generalizations for purposes of policy recommendations are tenuous. Additionally, most of the research has focused on deadly force and not force more broadly. The survey conducted by the Police Foundation provides the first national data that allows for an assessment of departmental policies, procedures, and practices and the use of force, and, in so doing, measures force broadly, encompassing both deadly and less than lethal force, and looks at sheriffs' departments, county police departments, and state agencies, as well as municipal departments.

D. DEPARTMENTAL POLICIES, PRACTICES, AND PROCEDURES AND THE RECEIPT AND DISPOSITION OF COMPLAINTS

The Independent Commission on LAPD was charged, after the Rodney King incident, to review policy and practice within the LAPD. This Commission claimed that, absent the video recording, the officers in the Rodney King incident would never have been held accountable for their behavior. The Commission report (1991) stated:

> The efforts of King's brother, Paul, to file a complaint were frustrated, and the report of the involved officers was falsified. Even if there had been an investigation, our case-by-case review of the handling of over 700 complaints indicates that without the Holliday videotape the complaint might have been adjudged to be "not sustained," because the officers' version conflicted with the account by King and his two passengers, who typically would have been viewed as not "independent."

Though limited empirical information is available, it appears there is wide variation among departments with regard to the rate of complaints received (see e.g., Kerstetter, 1985; Weitzer, 1986; Dugan and Breda, 1991). Similarly, there is much variation in the extent to which complaints are found to be true (see e.g., Culver, 1975, and Dugan and Breda, 1991). As indicated by the Rodney King example, however, the levels at which complaints are received and/or complaints are sustained may not be indicative of the amount of excessive force used by department members. The number of complaints filed with a department could be affected by factors such as the amount of faith that citizens put into the complaint review process and the ease with which complaints can be filed. Levels at which complaints are sustained may be affected by these same variables as well as by the quality of the investigation, the level of proof required to "sustain" a complaint, the existence of independent witnesses, the characteristics of the complainants, and so forth.

It is not surprising that when the police come under fire for misconduct, the processes for receiving and adjudicating complaints come under scrutiny. As reported in the 1967 Task Force Report on Police (President's Commission on Law Enforcement and Administration of Justice, hereafter referred to as the President's Commission): "How complaints should be handled and how misconduct should be dealt with has been the subject of perhaps the fiercest of the many controversies about the police that have raged in recent years" (1967: 193).

In this section we review what is known about how police departments receive and process complaints of police misconduct and how these procedures might affect rates of complaints received and the dispositions of those complaints. Most of the research reviewed has not focused specifically on excessive force complaints, but rather more broadly on complaints generally.

D.1 RATES AND TYPES OF COMPLAINTS

Several authors have provided rates of complaints received by various departments. Unfortunately, most of these studies have focused on a limited number of jurisdictions and the measures have not been consistent across studies, precluding cross-study comparisons. Walker and Bumphus (1992), citing a finding of the New York City Civilian Complaint Review Board (1990), reported that in 1990, misconduct complaints in New York City ranged from 1 per 10,000 police-citizen encounters to 5 per 10,000 police-citizen encounters, depending on the area of the city. Kerstetter (1985) calculated rates of complaints per officer for four cities using data collected by Perez (1978). Interestingly, the 1976 rates of complaints per officer for three of the cities—Kansas City, Oakland, and Chicago—were all .52:1. Berkeley's rate was higher at .95:1. Dugan and Breda (1991) received survey responses from 165 agencies in the state of Washington. The average number of complaints per year per agency was 4.2, or .27 per "public-contact enforcement officer in the agency" (p. 166). These researchers found no relationship between sizes of agencies and the rates of complaints or of sustained complaints.

Both Weitzer (1986) and Topping (1987) compared the rate of complaints in Northern Ireland to England and Wales. Both reported a far greater rate in Northern Ireland than in the other two countries. Topping (1987), for instance, found that the rate of complaints in Northern Ireland in 1985 was one per 500 persons in the population compared to one per 3,000 persons in England and Wales. Weitzer (1986) noted that Northern Ireland has two times the number of police officers per persons in the population and faces very different law enforcement challenges than those faced by either England or Wales.

Attempts to measure the extent to which a city receives complaints of misconduct can produce vastly different results depending on the source of data used. For instance, the Police Foundation publication, *The Big Six: Policing America's Largest Cities* (Pate and Hamilton, 1991) reported that police misconduct complaints received by the New York City Police Department, as reported by the department, in the years 1986 through 1990 ranged from approximately 5,000 to 10,000. In contrast, the "Police Brutality Study" conducted by the Criminal Section of the Civil Rights Division attempted to measure complaints of police misconduct against the New York City P.D. by relying on "complaints of official misconduct that were investigated by the Federal Bureau of Investigation and which were reported to the Civil Rights Division" (U.S. Department of Justice, Civil Rights Division, Criminal Section, 1991: p. 1). For 1986 through 1990, the Civil Rights Division reported between 6 and 23 complaints of police misconduct against New York City police officers.

Similar sporadic evidence is available regarding the types of complaints received by departments. Percentages of complaints that were excessive force complaints ranged from 17.5 in Dugan and Breda's (1991) study of 168 Washington State departments to 66.4 in "Metro City" studied by Wagner (1980a). Twenty-one percent of the misconduct complaints in Detroit in 1975 were for excessive force (Littlejohn, 1981). The corresponding figure for all five cities studied by Perez (1978) was 25 percent (Kerstetter, 1985), and in Northern Ireland the figure was 35 percent (Topping, 1987).

The other categories of complaints varied across studies, as they do across departments. Duga and Breda (1991) reported that 41.5 percent of the complaints to the Washington state agencies were for "verbal misconduct." In contrast, Wagner (1980a) reported that only 9.8 percent of the complaints against "Metro City" officers were for verbal abuse. Possibly Littlejohn's (1981) report of 24 percent "demeanor complaints" corresponds to the verbal misconduct category. Other categories reported by researchers are illegal arrest (at 15 percent in five cities, Kerstetter, 1985), illegal arrest or search and seizure (at 31 percent in Philadelphia in the early sixties, Coxe, 1961), harassment (at 26 percent in Philadelphia, Coxe, 1961), and procedure complaints (at 16 percent in Detroit in 1975, Littlejohn, 1981).

To add to what is known about the nature and extent of citizen complaints of excessive force, the Police Foundation survey collected information from the national sample of departments regarding the number of excessive force complaints received during 1991. The numbers of complaints, as well as the rates of complaints per number of sworn personnel, are presented in Chapter IV for the various agency types, sizes, and geographic locations.

D.2 CITIZEN CONFIDENCE IN AND AWARENESS OF THE COMPLAINT PROCESS

As mentioned above, the rate of complaints received by a jurisdiction may be as much a product of citizen confidence in the complaint process as any other factor. West (1988:113) commented that:

> Frequently assumed to provide a measure of police performance, the complaints rate is one of the most badly abused police-based statistics. Thus, an increasing number of complaints filed with a particular agency may not reflect a deterioration in standards of officer behavior, but could be interpreted as indicating a sign of increasing citizen confidence in the complaints system.

Similarly, Walker and Bumphus (1992) suggested that higher rates of complaints received by departments may reflect high citizen confidence in the investigation and disposition of complaints and thus argued that "a more open and responsive" system for processing complaints would likely lead to an increase in complaints. They reported (1992, citing Whitaker, 1982) that only one-third of the persons who believe they have been mistreated by police file complaints. They pointed out that this figure is not unlike the proportion of persons who report to the police the crimes committed against them. That 43 percent of those persons who did not report the mistreatment they perceived because it "wouldn't do any good" provides additional support for the contention that lack of citizen confidence in a complaint system will reduce the number of complaints received.

Additional support comes from case study data. As noted above, of the five cities studied by Perez (1978), Berkeley had the highest rate of complaints of police misconduct (see Kerstetter, 1985). The same study also found that the Berkeley complaint processing system was the most popular of the five. Conversely, Jolin and Gibbons (1984:p. 6) commenting on

Portland noted that "many citizens have no confidence in the [Internal Investigations Division] and its procedures, and are therefore reluctant to file complaints against the police."

Several researchers documented dramatic increases in complaints received by particular jurisdictions following revisions to the complaint review processes that seemed to be more open and responsive to the public. Littlejohn (1981), for instance, described the history of the Detroit Police-Community Relations Bureau, which was established in 1961 to, among other things, take over complaint investigation replacing the "decentralized precinct programs" (p. 25). Coinciding with the development of the new system and with other subsequent improvements to this unit, urged by Detroit's African American community, the number of complaints lodged by citizens increased over 200 percent between 1962 and 1968 (from 65 to 213). Subsequent to the creation of the civilian Board of Police Commissioners (BPC) in 1974, increases in complaints were again dramatic. The number of complaints received by this board in 1975 was twice the cumulative number received over the previous nine years! Littlejohn explained (1981:42): "Undoubtedly, the publicity which attended the creation of the BPC and its adoption of a grievance system which was generally perceived as credible accounts for the phenomenal increase in citizen complaint reports within one year."

Similarly dramatic was the increase in complaints from 200 per year to 100 per month in Philadelphia following modifications to the complaint review system and attendant publicity (Littlejohn, 1981). Also Walker and Bumphus (1992, citing Kahn, 1975) noted an "enormous" increase in complaints received by the New York City Police Department following changes to the complaint review process that made it "more open and more accessible to the public" (p. 9).

One aspect of this "openness" is the extent to which a department makes the public aware of the process by which to lodge complaints. Indeed, several studies (e.g., Jones et al., 1977, and Jones, 1980) found that citizens' propensity to contact government officials—for instance—to request a service or lodge a complaint, is a function of need for service and awareness of the systems and services of government. (Sharp (1984) found that need for service was the more important variable of the two.)

West (1988) found that 54 percent of the departments he studied gave out information to the public on the process for filing a complaint. Wagner and Decker (1993) found that brochures are "the most popular" form of advertising.

To address this aspect of the complaint process, the national survey collected information on the various ways departments make citizens in their jurisdictions aware of the complaint process. Additionally, information was collected about various other aspects of the complaint process that might indicate a more open and responsive system. These are discussed more fully in a subsequent section. The findings are presented in Chapter IV for each agency type, and for each agency type by size.

D.3 INTERNAL AND EXTERNAL COMPLAINT SYSTEMS

In many of the cities where citizens were dissatisfied with the complaint review process, systems incorporating civilian input were adopted, often at the insistence of the public (see e.g., Hudson, 1971; Littlejohn, 1981; Terrill, 1990). A department has "civilian review" if at some point in the complaint process persons other than sworn officers are involved (Walker and Bumphus, 1992). This can range from systems wherein citizens are involved with the investigation and review to systems where an individual citizen or citizen board is utilized only in instances in which there is citizen dissatisfaction with the departmental disposition (Walker and Bumphus, 1992).

Washington, D.C., established the first civilian review board in 1948 and was followed more than a decade later by boards that were developed in Philadelphia (1958), Minneapolis (1960), Rochester (1963), and New York City (1966) (see President's Commission, 1967; Littlejohn, 1981). Walker and Bumphus (1992) reported that by October of 1992, 68 percent of the 50 largest U.S. cities had some sort of civilian review. The practices in these large departments, however, are apparently not replicated within the smaller agencies. West (1988) surveyed a broader cross-section of departments and found that over 80 percent (83.9%) of the departments in the U.S. have "exclusively internal" processes for investigating complaints. Those with both external review and internal affairs units were more likely to be large (West, 1988: 112).

A number of authors have reviewed the positive and negative aspects of incorporating civilians into the complaint review process (see e.g., Gellhorn, 1966; Hudson, 1971; Terrill, 1982, 1990; Brown, 1983; and Hensley, 1988). Proponents of some form of civilian review argue that it is required to ensure objective investigation and disposition of complaints and to enhance the credibility of the process (see, e.g., American Civil Liberties Union, 1991). Additional arguments are that civilian participation will make the system appear less intimidating, and thus more accessible, provide for more thorough investigations, and provide for more appropriate dispositions of misconduct complaints (see e.g., Brown, 1983; Kerstetter, 1985; Skolnick and Fyfe, 1993).

Conversely, opponents claim that only law enforcement personnel have the expertise to evaluate the police behavior and that citizens have recourse in the forms of criminal prosecution or civil suit if they are not satisfied with the departmental review (see Terrill, 1982 and Brown, 1983). They express concern that the restraint imposed on police by an external review process would result in police becoming "so concerned about possible disciplinary action that they would be ineffective in their assigned duties" (Kerstetter, 1985:161).

A lot of what we know about civilian participation in the complaint process comes from case studies. The Philadelphia Board has received the most attention (see e.g., Bray, 1962; Coxe, 1961, 1965; Schwartz, 1970; Hudson, 1971; Hudson, 1972; Littlejohn, 1981), but the processes of other cities have been studied, as well. These include: New York (see e.g., Black, 1968; Hudson, 1971; Littlejohn, 1981; West, 1991), Detroit (Littlejohn, 1981; Terrill, 1982; West, 1991), Chicago (Letman, 1981; Terrill, 1982; West, 1991; Kerstetter and Van Winkle, 1989), Berkeley (Perez, 1978; Terrill, 1982; West, 1991), Kansas City (Terrill, 1982; West,

1991), and Portland (Jolin and Gibbons, 1984). Additionally, authors have looked at systems in Canada (see e.g., Barton, 1970; Watt, 1981; Goldsmith and Farson, 1987).

Providing a broader perspective are the results of a nationwide survey of civilian complaint systems reported in 1986 by the New York City Police Department Civilian Complaint Review Board (hereafter referred to as the New York City CCRB). The authors of this study divided complaint systems into three types: a completely internal system (that is, with no civilian involvement), an independent civilian or board charged with both the investigation and disposition of complaints and the "hybrid" system wherein the police department investigates the complaints, and the civilian entity provides some type of input to the system following investigation. (For other categorizations of internal and external complaint systems, see Littlejohn, 1981; Terrill, 1982; Peterson, 1991; and Walker and Bumphus, 1992.) The CCRB report compares the processes of the internal systems and the two civilian-involved systems in terms of intake, investigation, and disposition. For the most part, the systems do not differ appreciably except in terms of the civilian or sworn status of the actors at the various stages. As such, we discuss the stages of complaint processing below in a general fashion, combining information about internal and external systems, but indicating where differences exist.

The national survey collected information regarding the use of civilian review boards by departments across the country. Unlike previous surveys, the Police Foundation collected this information from small as well as large agencies, and from county police departments, sheriffs' departments, and state agencies, as well as from city police departments. The findings are presented in Chapter IV.

D.3.1 INTAKE

As indicated above, Rodney King's brother attempted to file a complaint of police misconduct on King's behalf but was frustrated in his attempt. This represents what happens when complaint intake processes place obstacles in the way of the citizens. At one time in San Francisco the counter at which complaints of police misconduct were filed had one inch squares of paper and a sign that read "Write your complaint here" (Schwartz, 1985). Though presumably a joke, this communication sent a message to citizens that complaints were not welcome.

Researchers have reviewed the intake processes at a number of departments. The Task Force Report (President's Commission, 1967), for instance, determined that jurisdictions used a variety of methods to discourage citizens from lodging complaints. A number of cities threatened complainants with criminal charges of false reports, and, in 1962, Washington, D.C., did in fact, so charge 40 percent of the complainants. The Task Force (President's Commission, 1967) reported that in Philadelphia in 1959 it was "standard practice" to charge all persons complaining of excessive force with resisting arrest or disorderly conduct. The practice in Washington, D.C., in 1966 was to bargain away the charges against the complainant if he or she dropped the complaint (President's Commission, 1967). In Boston, as late as 1964, a person detained in jail overnight, as a requirement for release, had to sign a paper indicating that he or she would not hold the police liable for any behavior related to the arrest (Fuller, 1964, as cited in Perez, 1978).

The Independent Commission on the LAPD heard testimony from citizens indicating that there were "significant hurdles" (1991:158) to filing a complaint. Some citizens said they were fearful, others indicated that the complaint process was "unnecessarily difficult or impossible" (1991:158). Evidence collected by the ACLU of Southern California indicated that the LAPD "actively discouraged the filing of complaints" (Walker and Bumphus, 1992: 11). Persons who phoned the department indicating that they needed to file complaints of police misconduct were infrequently referred to the toll-free number for filing of complaints (Walker and Bumphus, 1992).

The Management Review Committee of the Boston P.D. (St. Clair, 1992) reported that a number of community members who went to the police headquarters to file complaints of police misconduct were "discouraged" from doing so, others were apparently informed that no more forms were available.

The report on the L.A. Sheriff's Department indicated that "civilians attempting to lodge complaints at the charged officer's station are ignored, subjected to verbal abuse, and in some instances arrested" (Kolts, 1992:100). The team investigating the complaint process learned that citizens waited hours to receive the complaint forms they requested, Spanish-speaking complainants were erroneously told that complaints could only be lodged in English, and complainants were required to provide their driver's license numbers so that criminal record checks could be run on them.

Departments clearly vary in terms of the ease with which citizens can file complaints and some researchers have looked at policies regarding the receipt of complaints. Berel and Sisk (1964), for instance, received surveys from 191 of 544 cities serving 25,000 persons or more. They reported that the "normal practice" of these departments was to accept complaints by mail, by phone, or in person at either police headquarters or precinct stations. Three-fourths of the departments accepted anonymous complaints (e.g., by mail or phone). A decade later, Broadaway (1974) reported his results from a 1971 survey of 31 large cities regarding citizen complaint intake. Seven of the 31 (22.6%) only received complaints at police headquarters. The remaining 24 allowed for complaints to be filed at any police facility and some of those 24 allowed for complaints to be filed at alternative locations (e.g., with a review board), as well. Asked if they received complaints by mail, by phone and/or in person, 26 of 31 (83.9%) of the departments responded affirmatively to all three. Four of the 31 (12.9%) only received complaints if the citizen made it in person. Six of the 31 required that the citizen make a notarized statement.

Dempsey (1972) and West (1988) asked departments to indicate who could receive complaints. West reported that most of the departments he surveyed preferred that the initial report be taken by a supervisor. Most of the departments responding to Dempsey's survey reported that complaints could be received by "any superior officer"; the rest indicated that "any officer" could receive a complaint.

The New York City CCRB (1986) survey report indicated that almost all departments with internal complaint systems accepted complaints "24 hours a day, seven days a week, in person, by phone, or mail" (p. 3). Some departments provide for locations with "non-police atmospheres" where complaints can be lodged. Upon receipt of the complaint, a report is prepared to be forwarded to the investigating body.

The national survey conducted by the Police Foundation collected various types of information related to the intake stage of complaint processing, such as data on the methods by and locations at which citizens can file complaints and the time of day citizens can file complaints. Additionally, information was collected regarding the time limits for filing complaints, the assistance provided by departments to complainants, the requirements for filing complaints, and the persons authorized within departments to accept complaints. These results are presented in Chapter IV with comparisons of these policies and practices across the agency types and agency sizes.

D.3.2 INVESTIGATION

There is also variation across departments with regard to who investigates complaints. The U.S. Commission on Civil Rights (1981) suggested that a determination of the appropriate investigative body should be made on the basis of the following questions:

1. Who is in the best position to determine the facts honestly and without bias?
2. Who is best qualified to institute change?
3. Who has time available to investigate the allegations?

The National Advisory Commission on Criminal Justice Standards and Goals (1973) recommended that investigations of complaints of excessive or unnecessary force be handled by Internal Affairs Units. And indeed both the New York CCRB survey and the survey conducted by West (1988) indicated that the investigation is usually completed by officers in the Internal Affairs Division. Both surveys found that less serious complaints, however, were frequently investigated by the officer's division. The New York CCRB survey revealed that complaints are investigated in a manner consistent with any police investigation (1986:8):

> ...with statements taken, documentary evidence collected, and interrogation of subject and witness officers. The Fifth Amendment right of a subject officer is generally protected, either by allowing him/her to invoke the privilege, or guaranteeing that the statements made are not used in any subsequent criminal proceeding.

Kerstetter and Van Winkle (1989) studied Chicago complaints for 1985 and found that 40 percent of the cases had witnesses other than the complainant and the officer. Forty percent of these witnesses were fellow police officers and 32 percent were "related to or involved with" the complainant. Only 28 percent of the witnesses were "independent," that is, they were neither police officers nor related to or involved with the complainants.

Kerstetter and Van Winkle (1989) reported that 36 percent of the victims either refused to cooperate with the investigators (at the outset of the investigation or after the initial contact with investigators) or "could not be located or identified." Similarly, Walker and Bumphus (1992, citing New York City, 1990) reported that one-third of the complaints filed during a 12-month period in New York City were dropped because either the citizen withdrew the complaint or the citizen was unavailable or refused to cooperate with the investigation. Walker and Bumphus noted that this citizen behavior may be the result, at least in part, of investigators' behavior. They suggested that "complaint processing officials may discourage citizens through indifference, rudeness, or failure to act on complaints in a timely fashion" (p. 13).

West (1988) reported that just 18 percent of the departments surveyed investigated all complaints of police misconduct. The rest of the departments indicated that they screened cases prior to investigation. Sixty-four percent of the departments responding to West's survey had time limits on the processing of complaints. Of those departments, more than half had a 30-day time limit.

Several case studies of individual departments have provided valuable information regarding the investigation processes. Following their review of LAPD procedures, the Independent Commission recommended that all complaints of excessive force be handled by the Internal Affairs division and be subject to periodic audits by the police commission. The Independent Commission had found that the investigations conducted by the identified officers' divisions were inadequate. They found "for example, [that] in a number of complaint files ... there was no indication that the investigators had attempted to identify or locate independent witnesses, or if identified, to interview them" (1991:xix).

The Management Review Team of the Boston Police Department reported lengthy delays in the investigations of citizen complaints, insufficient "supervision or oversight to ensure thorough investigations" (p. 123) by the Internal Affairs unit, and "an appalling lack of documentation and record-keeping by IAD investigators" (St. Clair, 1992: 126).

The report on the L.A. Sheriff's Department indicated that a number of complaints were never investigated and that the investigations for a significant number of complaints were closed prior to completion "at times under highly suspicious circumstances" (Kolts, 1992:100). Those that were investigated were investigated in a "deficient" manner. In close to 100 of nearly 800 complaint files reviewed "there was no attempt to interview witnesses identified by LASD officers or the complainant" (Kolts, 1992:111).

The national survey conducted by the Police Foundation collected information from departments regarding the investigation of complaints. For instance, information was collected regarding the unit and individuals conducting investigations, safeguards for ensuring objectivity, time limits for investigating complaints, and officers' rights during the investigations. Additionally, information was collected regarding the existence and workings of Internal Affairs and Civilian Review units. These results are contained in Chapter IV.

D.3.3　ADMINISTRATIVE ROUTING

Following the investigation of a complaint, the report "may take a variety of administrative routes prior to final decisions on case finding and disposition being made" (West, 1988:106). The most common route, West reported, is from the investigator to the officer's supervisor through the officer's chain of command to the chief. Typically, the investigator makes the first recommendation regarding the disposition (e.g., as sustained, unfounded) and the supervisor makes the first recommendation on the appropriate discipline.

In Los Angeles, the disposition and penalty were initially determined by the charged officer's division commanding officer and then forwarded up a hierarchy that included area and bureau commanders, the Internal Affairs Division, and possibly the chief. Similar levels of review exist in other departments (see West, 1988, and the New York CCRB, 1986). The New York CCRB report found that "subject to civil service and other legal routes of appeal," authority to discipline officers is usually with the police chief or police commissioner. In some jurisdictions these decisions may be reviewed by the mayor, city manager, or city or county commission.

Departments completing the national survey of the Police Foundation provided information regarding who makes recommendations for disciplinary action on sustained complaints and who has the final responsibility for acting on the recommendations for disciplinary action.

D.3.4　DISPOSITIONS

Iannone (1987) outlined the typical categories of disposition used by departments. A "sustained" complaint is one that is supported by the facts. A complaint is "not sustained" if the evidence is insufficient to prove or disprove the allegations. If investigation determined that the act complained of did not occur—that is, the complaint was false—it is labeled "unfounded." The officer is "exonerated" if the act complained of did, in fact, occur but was legal, proper, and necessary.

Researchers examining the dispositions of complaints of police misconduct report sustained rates of between 0 and 25 percent. A figure of 10 percent or less appears to be the norm. The Task Force report (President's Commission, 1967) determined that fifty percent of departments sustained 10 percent or less of their complaints of misconduct. Culver (1975) compared the sustained rates of "Truck Stop City" to two other cities over a period encompassing 1972 and 1973. During that period, Los Angeles sustained 11 percent, New York 15 percent, and "Truck Stop City" zero percent (zero of 72 complaints). Wagner (1980a) studied "Metro City", a large urban area. He looked at 583 closed complaint files for the years 1971 and 1973 and found that only 5 percent were "sustained." (See also Decker and Wagner, 1982.) Two-thirds (68.6%) of the complaints were "not sustained," 16.5 percent were "unfounded," and in 9.9 percent of the cases the officers were exonerated.

Dugan and Breda (1991) found that 25 percent of the complaints received by the 165 Washington state agencies responding to their survey were sustained. For excessive force complaints, in particular, however, the sustained percentage was only 11.6 percent. This is consistent with the findings of Wagner (1980a), who found that excessive force complaints were the least likely to be sustained. The percent sustained of verbal misconduct complaints was 8.8 for 1971 and 1973, and for the "miscellaneous" category, the percent sustained was 11.5. In contrast, only 2.1 percent of the excessive force complaints were sustained. (See also Kerstetter and Van Winkle, 1989.) Box and Russell (1975) conjectured that the most serious complaints are the least likely to be sustained because they have the most severe consequences for the officer.

Weitzer (1986) determined that the percentage of complaints sustained in Northern Ireland was considerably lower than the corresponding percentages in England and Wales. The percent sustained in Northern Ireland between 1970 and 1985 ranged from .5 percent (in 1980) to 9 percent (in 1975). He explained low sustained rates generally as being a result of several factors: (1) there are corroborative witnesses only infrequently, making the case one of the word of the officer versus the word of the complainant; (2) officers do not admit their own guilt and they are likewise protected by their fellow officers, and (3) those charged with investigating and determining dispositions on complaints "tend to maintain a strong presumption of innocence" (p. 104).

Several researchers have attempted to link sustained rates to department characteristics. West (1988), for instance, reported that controlling for intake policies, departments with low numbers of complaints will have higher sustained rates. As Walker and Bumphus (1992) explained, low complaint rates may indicate that only the most serious complaints are being filed.

Perez (1978) studied the complaint systems of five departments and concluded that systems with civilian input are less likely to sustain complaints against officers than completely internal systems. On the other hand, the Philadelphia Police Department had no complaints sustained between 1952 and 1958, at which time a civilian review board was established. At the end of the second year, 107 complaints had been processed by the Board and 12 (11.2%) had been sustained.

Other researchers have looked at factors related to individual cases that might decrease the likelihood of the complaint being sustained. For instance, Kerstetter and Van Winkle (1989), studying Chicago, found that just 3.5 percent of the excessive force complaints received in 1985 were sustained. Over 80 percent were not sustained, 13.5 percent were unfounded, and in 1.8 percent of the cases the officer was exonerated. An important factor distinguishing sustained from not sustained was whether or not there was an "interactive arrest" of the complainant. An "interactive arrest" was an arrest resulting from "an interaction or altercation with a department member" (p. 4; e.g., resisting arrest, interfering with a police officer, disorderly conduct). Cases where there was an interactive arrest of the complainant were less likely to result in a sustained complaint than cases where there was no interactive arrest. A major factor determining whether or not the facts were established one way or another—that is, there was a determination of complaint sustained or officer exonerated—was the existence of independent corroborating evidence (e.g., an independent witness).

The Independent Commission on the LAPD found that only 42 of 2,152 (2.0%) excessive force complaints filed between 1986 and 1990 in the city of Los Angeles were sustained. The Commission explained that it was "rare" to have a complaint of excessive force sustained "unless there are non-involved, independent witnesses who corroborate the complainant's version of the facts" (1991:155). Conversely, "non-sustained" was the disposition for cases where the only witnesses were the officer and the complainant, or witnesses for the complainant which were not "non-involved and independent." The report claimed that "the Department's system of classification (was) ... biased in favor of officers charged with excessive force or improper tactics" (1991:162).

The Special Counsel investigating the L.A. Sheriff's Department found, however, that even citizen complaints that were "corroborated by physical evidence and independent witnesses" were frequently not sustained (Kolts, 1992: 100). Of 670 allegations of excessive force generated between 1990 and April 1992 (excluding those pending), 46 percent were deemed "unfounded" (i.e., untrue), 35 percent were deemed "unsubstantiated" (i.e., there was insufficient evidence for a conclusion), and 6 percent were "founded" (Kolts, 1992:99). The investigations of the remaining 14 percent were closed prior to completion. Interestingly, the Special Counsel team found vastly differing perceptions on the part of departmental personnel regarding the applicable level of proof for proving allegations of misconduct.

The Management Review Committee of the Boston Police Department found that from 1989 to 1990 the percentages of all complaints (not just excessive force complaints) that were sustained decreased from 11 percent to 3 percent. Conversely, the percentage of complaint cases that were not sustained increased from 45 percent to 70 percent across the same two years. The Committee commented that these figures may indicate a "disturbing trend" in which "the Department's internal review process seems increasingly less likely to believe citizens filing complaints (and less likely to) find fault with their own personnel" (St. Clair, 1992: 107).

Box and Russell (1975) used data from two police forces in England and Wales to determine whether "discrediting" characteristics of complainants were related to the dispositions in cases. To do this, they compared the sustained rates across complainants differing in terms of their social class and whether or not they were arrested during the incidents, whether or not they had prior records, whether or not they evidenced signs of mental illness, and whether or not they were under the influence of drugs or alcohol at the time of the incidents. First of all, the researchers found that "working class complainants," complainants with criminal records, complainants who had been arrested during the encounters that led to the complaints, persons with signs of mental illness, and persons who were under the influence of alcohol during the encounters were all less likely to have their complaints sustained. The researchers also created an index of "discredits" made up of the variables: prior arrest, arrest during encounter, prosecution for arrest during encounter, mental illness, and drunkenness and found that none of the complainants with two or more "discredits" had his/her complaint sustained. Ten percent of those with one "discredit," and 40 percent of those with no "discredits" had their complaints sustained. Chevigny (1969) has suggested that officers are more likely to misbehave with "discredited" or otherwise less powerful citizens, because of the reduced likelihood that these citizens' complaints will be believed.

The national survey conducted by the Police Foundation collected information regarding the dispositions of excessive force complaints received by departments during 1991. Additionally, information was collected regarding the characteristics of persons who filed complaints and of the persons whose complaints were sustained. In Chapter IV we describe the dispositions of excessive force complaints. That is, we provide information regarding the proportions of complaints received that were sustained, those that were not sustained, those that were determined to be unfounded, and those in which the officers were exonerated. Further, we compare the characteristics of three groups of citizens: a) citizens in the jurisdictions of the law enforcement agencies, b) citizens who filed complaints, and c) citizens whose complaint allegations were sustained. We discuss the characteristics that distinguish the three groups.

D.3.5   SANCTIONS

The United States Commission on Civil Rights (1981:71) noted that "the most thorough mechanisms for detecting officer misconduct will be without effect unless the proven misconduct is accompanied by appropriate sanctions that are both swift and certain." Similarly, the Police Foundation, in a publication on deadly force (Milton, et al., 1977:65), addressed this issue:

> Enforcement is the ultimate test. What happens to the officer who indefensibly disobeys a policy? If nothing happens (or nothing very dramatic), the policy is just another piece of paper among many. If such an officer is fired, suspended, demoted, or otherwise seriously disciplined, the disciplinary action is an important indication that the policy is in fact a policy.

In the late sixties, the Task Force (President's Commission, 1967:197) concluded, based on a survey conducted by Michigan State University, that "probably the strongest criticism that can be offered is that seldom is meaningful disciplinary action taken against officers guilty of one or more of the forms of brutality." However, they also found a few departments that gave particularly harsh sanctions for even minor violations.

Culver (1975) studying a single city found that of 40 sustained complaints, 12 resulted in verbal reprimands, 3 in written reprimands, and 12 in suspensions (for 1 day to 2 months). Perez (1978) based on his comparison of complaint review systems in five cities claimed that civilian systems were more lenient in terms of discipline than internal systems.

The Independent Commission on the LAPD reported that not only are few allegations of police use of excessive force sustained, but those that are sustained are given punishment "more lenient than it should be" (1991:165). One deputy chief interviewed by the commission expressed the belief that punishments were more harsh for violations that embarrassed the department than for behavior that harmed citizens. The commission reported that support for this view came from members of the Police Protective League and "many patrol officers" (p. 166).

The Independent Commission recommended that officers with sustained excessive force complaints receive appropriately harsh punishments as well as training and counseling. The report stated (1991:177): "It is not enough to punish those who use excessive force, and hope that it does not happen again. The Department must take affirmative steps to ensure that the officer will modify his or her behavior." Additionally, the commission recommended that the city charter be modified to allow for the punishment of supervisors where appropriate.

The Special Counsel team investigating the L.A. Sheriff's Department determined that, in those rare instances when an excessive force complaint was sustained, the discipline imposed was frequently "far too lenient" (Kolts, 1992:119). In most instances, departmental discipline for sustained allegations of excessive force was between one and five days' suspension.

Information from the national survey is presented in Chapter IV regarding the sanctions received by officers against whom excessive force complaints were sustained. Specifically, for each agency type, and for each agency type by size, we indicate the extent to which the subject of sustained complaints were disciplined by reprimand, reassignment, suspension, or termination.

D.3.6   FOLLOW-UP

West (1988) reported that most of the departments he studied allow both officer and complainant to appeal the disposition of a complaint and allow the officer to appeal the discipline imposed. Further, West explained that most departments inform the complainant of the disposition in the case, but not the form of discipline imposed, if any. Berel and Sisk (1964) found that only 5 percent of the departments surveyed would give the complainant a copy of the report on request.

Finally, West (1988) found that 54 percent of the departments he surveyed publish information regarding the number of complaints received and the disposition of those cases. Most frequently, this information is contained in the chief's annual report.

Departments responding to the national survey indicated whether the officer, the citizen, or both had a right to appeal the disposition of a complaint. They also indicated whether or not complaint information was published and made available to the public. These results are presented in Chapter IV.

E.   CONCLUSIONS

As described in this chapter, a number of studies have taken on the difficult task of examining the use of reasonable force and excessive force by police, as well as departmental policies, procedures, and practices related to the use of both types of force. Each study, though valuable, has certain limitations. Most of the data from the major observational studies on the use of force—which have been collected or analyzed in a secondary fashion by Black and Reiss (1967), Friedrich (1977, 1980), Worden (1992)—were collected prior to 1980. Further, though these studies are a valuable source of individual and situational information related to the use of force by police, they suffer from the potential for officer reactivity to the observation and usually only provide a limited number of cases from which to generalize.

Data concerning allegations of excessive force from alternative complaint agencies—such as that collected by Chevigny (1969)—are instructive, as well, in understanding the individual and situational characteristics of complaints, but are not necessarily representative of either excessive force incidents or of excessive force complaints. As mentioned previously, the study conducted by the Criminal Section of the Civil Rights Division of the U.S. Department of Justice (1991) relied on data consisting of complaints of police misconduct which were reported to the federal authorities and investigated by the FBI. Unfortunately, the data which were used not for this study only suffer from being based only on *reported* cases, but are based on cases reported to a grievance procedure of which most people are not aware and which applies to only a small range of the total types of complaints that can be made against police misconduct.

Data from community surveys on the incidence and prevalence of police use of force can tap into unreported incidents of excessive force in the way official records cannot. However, these surveys measure only individual perceptions of excessive force, and not necessarily force that is legally defined as excessive.

Studies of law enforcement agencies, which focus on citizen complaints of police misconduct or the complaint review process, have provided some valuable preliminary information. However, these studies have generally examined just one or a few departments or one narrow aspect of the issues.

Recognizing their strengths and weakness, we have utilized this previous research to focus the national survey undertaken by the Police Foundation. That survey was developed to fill some of the major gaps in our knowledge regarding the extent to which police use force, the reporting requirements regarding those incidents of use of force, the extent to which citizens complain that excessive force is used, the nature of departmental mechanisms to solicit and process those complaints, characteristics of complainants and officers against whom complaints are lodged, the disposition of those complaints, and the disciplinary action taken on those complaints found to be sustained. As such, this study has produced the most comprehensive data base ever assembled on the issue of police use of force and complaints of excessive force.

In the next chapter, we describe the methods used to conduct the national survey. In the fourth chapter, we present the major results of the survey. The fifth chapter summarizes and discusses these findings.

III. Methods

This chapter of the report describes the methods used to conduct this study. The first part of the chapter describes how the law enforcement agency questionnaire was constructed, explains how the agency sample was selected, specifies how the survey was conducted, and provides a description of selected characteristics of the agencies that responded to the survey. The second part describes how the data were analyzed. The third part of the chapter discusses the methodological limitations of the study. The final part provides a summary overview of the reliability and validity of the research findings.

A. The Law Enforcement Agency Survey

A.1 Questionnaire Construction

The first task in questionnaire construction was the development of a topical conceptual outline based upon a thorough review of the literature concerning police use of force. This outline was used as the basis for the framework upon which to structure the first draft of an instrument. After extensive review and revisions, a refined version of this questionnaire was reviewed by several researchers, practitioners, and staff of the National Institute of Justice. This review included a one-day focus group meeting with practitioners from five law enforcement agencies in the Washington, D.C., metropolitan area. After changes resulting from this review were incorporated, another version of the questionnaire was sent to a pretest sample of eighteen law enforcement agencies of various types, sizes, and geographical locations. In addition to completing the questionnaire, the agencies included in the pretest were requested to provide assistance in clarifying the terms, improving the structure, and reducing the length of the questionnaire. One of the most important results of this preliminary work was the discovery that, in order to maximize the chances for cooperation, agencies had to be provided with the assurance that their responses would not be associated with their identities.

Based on the results of the pretest, a 20-page questionnaire (including instructions and a glossary) was created. This instrument, a copy of which is included as Appendix A of this report, solicits information regarding reported use of force of various types, citizen complaints of excessive force, the disposition of those complaints, as well as litigation concerning allegations of excessive force. In addition, the questionnaire requests information concerning agency size, demographic characteristics, workload, policies and procedures, and other topics. In keeping with the findings of the pretest, agencies were assured that their responses would be kept confidential.

A.2 Selecting the Sample

In order to obtain a representative sample of law enforcement agencies, the Police Foundation obtained a copy of the Law Enforcement Sector portion of the 1990 Justice Agency List from the Governments Division of the Bureau of the Census, the most complete and exhaustive enumeration of such agencies available. This list, the one from which the sample for the periodic Law Enforcement Management and Administrative Statistics survey is drawn by the Bureau of Justice Statistics, is more comprehensive than the list of agencies maintained by the Uniform Crime Reports program of the Federal Bureau of Investigation, which contains information only about those agencies that participate in that program. The Justice Agency List contained information concerning the agency type, the type of government served, the 1990 population of the jurisdiction served by each agency, and the number of employees in each agency in 1987.

From among the 17,708 agencies on the Law Enforcement Sector list, 15,801 were found to be county sheriffs' departments, county police departments, municipal police departments, or state agencies. The distribution of those agencies, categorized by the size of the jurisdiction they served in 1990 (50,000 and over; 25,000 to 49,999; 10,000 to 24,999; or below 10,000), is shown in Table 1.

As Table 1 indicates, over 66 percent of law enforcement agencies of all types served jurisdictions with fewer than 10,000 persons; 9 percent of the agencies served jurisdictions with 50,000 or more inhabitants. Among municipal police departments, the disparity is even more dramatic, with over 77 percent of the agencies serving jurisdictions below 10,000 and approximately 4 percent serving those with 50,000 and over. The majority of sworn officers, however, are employed by the agencies in the largest jurisdictions. As shown by the latest estimates provided by the Law Enforcement Management and Administrative Statistics (LEMAS) survey (Reaves, 1992a, 1992b), 15.3 percent of the sworn personnel in municipal police departments worked in agencies serving jurisdictions of below 10,000 persons; almost 61 percent worked in agencies serving jurisdictions with 50,000 or more inhabitants. Among sheriffs' departments, only 3 percent of the sworn officers worked in agencies serving jurisdictions of below 10,000 persons, while 79 percent worked for jurisdictions of 50,000 or more persons.

As a result of the fact that a large majority of law enforcement officers work in a relatively small minority of agencies serving large jurisdictions, it was important, in selecting the sample, to ensure adequate representation of agencies serving larger jurisdictions, even though they accounted for a small number of the total. To do so, a stratified sampling procedure was used to select agencies within jurisdiction size categories. Among municipal police departments, all agencies serving jurisdictions of 50,000 inhabitants or more were selected for the sample, along with a random sample of 20 percent of the agencies serving between 25,000 and 49,999 persons, a random sample of 10 percent of agencies serving jurisdictions of 10,000 to 24,999 persons, and a random sample of 2 percent of the agencies serving below 10,000 inhabitants.

Among county agencies, including sheriffs' departments and county police departments, all agencies serving jurisdictions of 100,000 inhabitants or more were selected for the sample. A random sample of the remaining agencies was selected as follows: 20 percent of agencies serving between 50,000 and 99,999 persons, 10 percent of agencies serving between 25,000 and 49,999 persons, and 2 percent of agencies serving below 25,000 inhabitants.

Because of their small number, all state agencies on the Census list were included in the sample.

TABLE 1

**Universe of Law Enforcement Agencies
by Agency Type and Population of Jurisdiction Served**

Population Served	Agency Type				
	County Sheriffs' Dept.	County Police Dept.	Municipal Police Dept.	State Police Agency	Total
50,000 and over	794 (26.2)	47 (78.3)	535 (4.2)	53 (100.0)	1,429 (9.0)
25,000 to 49,999	607 (20.1)	5 (8.3)	690 (5.4)	0 (0.0)	1,302 (8.2)
10,000 to 24,999	905 (29.9)	5 (8.3)	1,668 (13.2)	0 (0.0)	2,578 (16.3)
Below 10,000	721 (23.8)	3 (5.0)	9,768 (77.2)	0 (0.0)	10,492 (66.4)
Total	3,027 (100.0)	60 (100.0)	12,661 (100.0)	53 (100.0)	15,801 (100.0)

NOTE: Numbers in parentheses represent column percents

TABLE 2

Sample of Eligible Law Enforcement Agencies
by Agency Type and Population of Jurisdiction Served

Population Served	Agency Type				
	County Sheriffs' Dept.	County Police Dept.	Municipal Police Dept.	State Police Agency	Total
50,000 and over	479 (81.5)	43 (100.0)	527 (51.9)	50 (100.0)	1,099 (64.8)
25,000 to 49,999	67 (11.4)	0 (0.0)	139 (13.7)	0 (0.0)	206 (12.1)
10,000 to 24,999	23 (3.9)	0 (0.0)	174 (17.1)	0 (0.0)	197 (11.6)
Below 10,000	19 (3.2)	0 (0.0)	176 (17.3)	0 (0.0)	195 (11.5)
Total	588 (100.0)	43 (100.0)	1,016 (100.0)	50 (100.0)	1,697 (100.0)

NOTE: Numbers in parentheses represent column totals

After the stratification procedure was applied, a total sample of 1,725 agencies was selected from the list provided by the Census Bureau. Upon further scrutiny, it was determined that 28 of those agencies selected were ineligible for the survey, 17 because they were not law enforcement agencies, five because they no longer existed, and six (including three state agencies) because they were each listed twice in the directory. Table 2 shows the distribution of the 1,697 eligible agencies that remained in the sample.

A.3 CONDUCTING THE SURVEY

The initial mailing of the survey took place in mid-August of 1992. Each survey package contained a cover letter, questionnaire, a return envelope, and a postcard, which the departments were to return to the Police Foundation upon receipt of the packet indicating the person within each department completing the survey. The first follow-up, in early September, took the form of a faxed letter to those departments that had not returned either a postcard or survey. Six weeks after the initial mailing, departments that had not returned either a completed questionnaire or the postcard were sent another package containing a survey and a revised cover letter. Telephone calls were made to the departments that had returned postcards but not questionnaires.

A total of 1,111 completed questionnaires were received, placed into computer-readable format, and analyzed. Table 3 provides an analysis of the survey response results by agency type. As that table shows, these 1,111 questionnaires represent an overall response rate of 67.2 percent. This includes 72.4 percent of the municipal police departments, 88.9 percent of the county police departments, 54.2 percent of the sheriffs' departments, and 90.0 percent of the state agencies.

A.4 THE AGENCY SAMPLE

Table 4 provides information about the size of the populations of jurisdictions served by the 1,111 responding agencies, according to their type. In parentheses, under the absolute numbers, are the percentage of agencies in each size category that provided responses. As the table reveals, the highest percentage of responses was achieved for the agencies serving the largest jurisdictions, regardless of agency type. Among sheriffs' departments, for example, 52.4 percent of the sampled agencies serving jurisdictions of 50,000 or more persons provided responses, compared to 42.1 percent of those serving jurisdictions with fewer than 10,000 persons. Similarly, among municipal police departments, 80.3 percent of the sampled agencies serving jurisdictions of 50,000 persons and over responded, compared to 58.0 percent of those serving jurisdictions with below 10,000 persons. Analyses of these differences indicate that they do not reach the .05 level of statistical significance.

The distribution of the responding agencies, by agency size and type, are shown in Table 5.

TABLE 3

Survey Response Results by Agency Type

Agency Type	Sample	Complete	Refuse	Ineligible	No Response	Other*	Response Rate**
Municipal Police	1,016 (100.0)	731 (71.9)	57 (5.6)	3 (0.3)	221 (21.8)	4 (0.4)	72.4
County Police	43 (100.0)	32 (74.4)	1 (2.3)	4 (9.3)	3 (7.0)	3 (7.0)	88.9
County Sheriff	588 (100.0)	303 (51.5)	51 (8.7)	28 (4.8)	205 (34.9)	1 (0.2)	54.2
State Police	50 (100.0)	45 (90.0)	1 (2.0)	0 (0.0)	4 (8.0)	0 (0.0)	90.0
Total	1,697 (100.0)	1,111 (65.5)	110 (6.5)	35 (2.1)	433 (25.5)	8 (0.5)	67.2

NOTE: Numbers in parentheses represent row percents

TABLE 4

Number and Percentage of Responding Law Enforcement Agencies by Agency Type and Population of Jurisdiction Served

Population Served	Agency Type				
	County Sheriffs' Dept.	County Police Dept.	Municipal Police Dept.	State Police Agency	Total
50,000 and over	251 (52.4)	32 (74.4)	423 (80.3)	45 (90.0)	751 (68.3)
25,000 to 49,999	34 (50.7)	0 (0.0)	99 (71.2)	0 (0.0)	132 (64.1
10,000 to 24,999	10 (43.5)	0 (0.0)	107 (61.5)	0 (0.0)	117 (56.8)
Below 10,000	8 (42.1)	0 (0.0)	102 (58.0)	0 (0.0)	111 (56.9)
Total	303 (51.5)	32 (74.4)	731 (71.9)	45 (90.0)	1,111 (65.5)

NOTE: Numbers in parentheses represent the percent of agencies responding

TABLE 5

**Responding Law Enforcement Agencies
by Agency Type and Number of Sworn Personnel**

Sworn Personnel	Agency Type				
	County Sheriffs' Dept.	County Police Dept.	Municipal Police Dept.	State Police Agency	Total
1000 and over	9 (3.0)	2 (6.2)	29 (4.0)	16 (35.6)	56 (5.0)
500 to 999	15 (5.0)	(4) (12.5)	32 (4.4)	13 (28.9)	64 (5.8)
250 to 499	31 (10.2)	10 (31.2)	68 (9.3)	10 (22.2)	119 (10.7)
100 to 249	69 (22.8)	5 (15.6)	207 (28.3)	6 (13.3)	287 (25.8)
50 to 99	78 (25.7)	6 (18.8)	155 (21.2)	0 (0.0)	239 (21.5)
25 to 49	49 (16.2)	3 (9.4)	109 (14.9)	0 (0.0)	161 (14.5)
1 to 24	52 (17.2)	2 (6.3)	131 (17.9)	0 (0.0)	185 (16.7)
Total	303 (100.0)	32 (100.0)	731 (100.0)	45 (100.0)	1,111 (100.0)

NOTE: Numbers in parentheses represent column percents

B. DATA ANALYSIS

The research project presented in this report sought to collect, describe, and analyze data concerning the reported use of force by police, citizen complaints of excessive force, and legal consequences of allegations of excessive force. In the next chapter, the information collected will be presented so as to provide comparisons across different types of law enforcement agencies, and, for municipal police departments and sheriffs' departments, to compare agencies of different sizes.

B.1 RATIONALE

The comparisons across agency type are presented because, given the considerable differences in structure, mission, workload, constituency, and other factors (see Reaves, 1992, for basic comparisons across agency type), it could be expected that the use of force, and procedures for responding to it, would differ among the four types.

Comparisons across agency size are provided because, even within agencies of the same type, the nature of the job of a law enforcement officer, and the organizational environment within which such an officer must work, can be expected to vary widely, depending on the size of the agency. Weisheit, Falcone, and Wells (1993), in their comprehensive review of rural policing, for example, have pointed out that small agencies differ from larger ones in terms of geographic isolation, number of officers per vehicle, differential access to medical treatment, gun ownership, presence of formal policies, familiarity with suspects, and other factors that might affect the use of force. Slovak (1986), relying on the previous work of Hage (1980), focuses more specifically on organizational differences between large and small agencies, particularly differentiation of work tasks and intensity of supervision.

B.2 GROUPING OF RESPONSES

Comparisons across agency sizes are made by presenting, within each agency type, the appropriate measure obtained within each agency size category. To provide the most robust estimates, no size category indicators were utilized unless they were based on the responses of at least 20 agencies. For example, because fewer than 20 responses were received from sheriffs' departments in size categories with 500 to 999 and 1,000 and over sworn officers, those two categories were combined with the 250 to 499 size category to create a 250 or more category. Because of the small sample sizes among county police departments and state agencies, no agency size analyses were conducted for those agency types. (Complete results, containing unweighted and ungrouped indicators, are provided in Appendix B of this report.)

B.3 WEIGHTING

As mentioned previously, sampling was conducted after stratifying by agency type and size of jurisdiction. As a result, the distribution of agencies responding to the survey overrepresents the number of agencies in large jurisdictions, compared to their presence in the nation in general. In addition, as the preceding section reveals, larger agencies were somewhat more likely to respond to the survey than were smaller ones. To compensate for the stratified sampling and differential response, analyses in this report comparing agency types are made by presenting means, percentages, or rates that have been weighted to reflect the distribution, by agency size, found in the universe of agencies. To provide these weighted estimates, the responses to each question were categorized according to the number of sworn officers in the responding agency (1 to 24, 25 to 49, 50 to 99, 100 to 249, 250 to 499, 500 to 999, and 1,000 or more). The responses from each category were then weighted according to their percentage distribution among all agencies of that type, as estimated by the Law Enforcement Management and Administrative Statistics (LEMAS) survey, conducted by the Bureau of Justice Statistics (Reaves, 1992a, 1992b, 1993).

For example, as a result of the combination of the stratified sampling procedure utilized in the survey and the differential response rate across agency sizes, city police departments with 1,000 or more sworn officers accounted for 4.0 percent of the responding agencies; agencies with fewer than 25 sworn officers accounted for 17.9 percent of those responding. Among all municipal agencies, on the other hand, those with 1,000 or more sworn officers accounted for 0.3 percent; those with fewer than 25 officers made up 79.0 percent. So that the distribution of responding agencies would be the same as that among all agencies, the responses have been weighted so that their distribution is equal to that estimated in the LEMAS survey. Thus, among municipal agencies, the responses provided by those with fewer than 25 officers were weighted .79, those with 1,000 or more officers were weighted .03, etc. Because virtually the entire universe of state agencies responded to the survey, no weighting was applied to those responses.

The application of such a weighting procedure ensures that the distributions, by size, of the agencies for which data is presented in this study resemble the distributions estimated to exist among each agency type in the nation as a whole. Such weighting, however, cannot compensate for the possibility that the agencies that responded to the survey may differ, in one or more significant, but unmeasured ways, from those that did not respond. It is possible, for example, that agencies responding to the survey were more likely to have accurate record keeping systems, have rigorous systems for monitoring and controlling the use of force, or manifest different management styles, than were agencies not providing such data. Such differences cannot be expected to be accounted for simply by weighting by agency size.

Furthermore, as will be seen in the next chapter, varying numbers of agencies responded to the survey but were unable or unwilling to provide data concerning certain issues, including the extent of the use of various types of force, the number and disposition of citizen complaints of excessive force, as well as information concerning civil suits and criminal charges. It is likewise possible that agencies providing such data may differ substantially from those that did not.

As a result, even though the response rate for the survey was gratifyingly high, until further research is conducted to compare the characteristics of the responding agencies to those that did not respond, generalizations from the results of this survey to all law enforcement agencies should be made with caution.

B.4 TESTS OF STATISTICAL SIGNIFICANCE

All comparisons of categorical variables have included tests of the statistical significance of differences, if any. All means have likewise been subjected to significance testing appropriate to their level of measurement. The results of these tests have been taken into account in interpreting the results of the various comparisons presented in this report. Such tests, however, are heavily influenced by sample size, making small differences among large samples likely to be found significant while large differences among small samples likely not to be found significant. In addition, as pointed out by Morrison and Henkel in their classic, *The Significance Test Controversy*, such tests are subject to misinterpretation and misuse. Recognizing the limits of such tests, the authors did not use them as the sole criterion by which differences were assessed. Instead, following the sage advice of Hans Zeisel, a mentor of one of the authors, we have also sought to pay attention to the "significance of insignificant differences." As Zeisel stated almost 40 years ago:

> There is now, in the social sciences, no greater need than the development of theoretical insights guided by empirical data. At such times, to provide this guidance and service as a stimulant is the significance of statistically insignificant data. Even if the probability is great that an inference will have to be rejected later, the practical risk of airing it is small. Subsequent and more elaborate studies may disprove some of these inferences; but for those that survive, social science will be the richer (Zeisel, reprinted in Morrison and Henkel, 1970, p. 80).

We believe the status of research on police use of force is in need of "the development of theoretical insights guided by empirical data." Thus, in the discussion that follows, although we have paid attention to those differences that reached the .05 level of statistical significance, we have also recognized that some of those differences reached that level primarily because of the large number of cases being examined. On the other hand, we have brought attention to differences that, although not reaching the typical standard of statistical significance, appeared to us, based on our experience, to merit further attention and discussion. All other readers are invited to apply their own criteria (and their own experience) to the raw data and significance tests in order to reach their own conclusions.

C. LIMITATIONS OF THE STUDY

As discussed in the review of the literature, all previous research on the topic of police use of force has had limitations. This study has sought to correct for a number of those limitations. Unlike observational studies, for example, this study has not been restricted to a small number of encounters between police and citizens. Unlike surveys of citizens, this study has not relied on the perceptions or attitudes of the general population or of those who have had contact with the police. Unlike case studies, this research has not been limited to a small number of agencies.

Nevertheless, this research itself has limitations that should be taken into account when evaluating its reliability and validity. Specifically, the data upon which this study is based are derived from the responses (a) to a mail survey, (b) requiring self-administered responses, (c) provided by organizational representatives selected by the agencies themselves, (d) concerning topics considered by some law enforcement agencies to be sensitive. As such, it suffers from the limitations of mail surveys, self-administered questionnaires, agency surveys, and all inquiries concerning sensitive topics. Each of these limitations will be discussed below.

C.1 LIMITATIONS OF MAIL SURVEYS

As described by a number of survey experts (see, for example, Warwick and Lininger, 1975; Dillman, 1978, 1983; and Babbie, 1990), mail surveys have historically demonstrated a number of problems. A common limitation of such surveys has been that the mailing lists from which the samples were drawn were incomplete or out of date. As mentioned above, great precautions have been taken in this study to obtain and update the most complete and current list of law enforcement agencies available. Nevertheless, the possibility should be acknowledged that the list from which the sample was drawn may have omitted some eligible agencies.

A second disadvantage of mail surveys has been that such surveys have traditionally suffered from lower response rates than those obtained by conducting interviews face-to-face or by telephone. Effective approaches have been developed, however, that greatly enhance the response rates of such surveys (see Warwick and Lininger, 1975; Dillman, 1978, 1983). This study has used such approaches, including providing stamped, self-addressed return envelopes; giving suggested deadline dates; sending faxes as reminders; making frequent follow-up telephone calls; and other such techniques, to produce a response rate of almost 70 percent, considered, according to Babbie's "rule of thumb," as "very good" for such efforts (1990: 182).

Despite this relatively high response rate, approximately 30 percent of the sampled agencies did not complete and return the questionnaire. Furthermore, a number of agencies failed to provide responses to particular items on that questionnaire, particularly those involving the use of various types of force, citizen complaints of excessive force, and civil suits and criminal charges. As a result, despite the fact that the responses have been weighted to reflect the size distribution of the nation's law enforcement agencies, generalization to all agencies would not be appropriate, because agencies that did not respond may differ from those that did.

C.2 LIMITATIONS OF SELF-ADMINISTERED QUESTIONNAIRES

Self-administered questionnaires pose problems not presented by those administered by interviewers (Dillman, 1983). Completing such questionnaires, for example, requires literacy skills not needed when responding orally to an interview. In addition, it is especially difficult, using self-administered questionnaires, to obtain information in an open-ended format, by means of screeners, or in a particular sequence. Lengthy questionnaires, especially those that request complex data, are also difficult to complete using the self-administration approach.

The pre-test was used in this study as a means of minimizing the extent to which all of these difficulties were encountered. Terminology was kept as simple as possible; a glossary of terms was included to provide common definitions. Open-ended responses and screeners were used only when absolutely necessary. The length of the questionnaire was reduced to be as brief as possible, while still obtaining the necessary data. Despite all of these precautions, the questionnaire, in order to provide useful information, demanded the conscientious attention of those responding to it.

In addition, as with all self-administered questionnaires, the one used in this study ran the risk that the person or persons responding may, consciously or unconsciously, not have provided complete and accurate information. This could be due, for instance, to faulty human memory, inadequate agency records, or respondents' attempts to portray their agencies in the best possible light.

C.3 LIMITATIONS OF AGENCY QUESTIONNAIRES

Many contemporary law enforcement agencies are besieged by rising crime, declining staffing levels, and restricted budgets. To expect such agencies to expend the time and energy necessary to complete yet another questionnaire in the midst of such circumstances was optimistic in the extreme. The fact that almost 70 percent of the eligible agencies sampled provided responses is a tribute to their professionalism. Nevertheless, it should be recognized that, because of conflicting demands, some agencies were unable to respond because they did not have the resources to do so.

Furthermore, although the questionnaire utilized in this research was sent to the chief executive of each agency selected to participate, it was to be expected that the actual responses to that instrument would be provided, in many cases, by a person or persons other than the chief executive. This expectation was confirmed by an analysis of the responses provided on the returned questionnaires concerning the identity of the persons who completed them. Respondents included chief executives, senior administrators, heads of various types of units, as well as lieutenants, sergeants, and patrol officers. Weiss (1992) has demonstrated that significantly different responses can be provided by different persons, representing different organizational points of view, within the same law enforcement agency.

Because it was impossible to control the method by which the questionnaire was distributed within the sampled agencies, it is not possible to be certain why particular persons were selected to complete the instrument, how they obtained the information provided, how complete and accurate that information was, or what motivation lay behind the provision of that information. Interpretation of the data analyzed in this report, therefore, must be undertaken with those uncertainties in mind.

C.4 LIMITATIONS OF SURVEYS OF SENSITIVE TOPICS

As demonstrated in the review of the literature, the issues of police use of force, allegations of excessive force, and the legal consequences of such allegations, are sensitive ones for many law enforcement agencies. McLaughlin (1992), in his summary of some of the problems doing research on the issue of use of force by police, noted that law enforcement agencies may resist providing information about the use of force by their officers because of fear of damaging the reputation of the agency, a general unwillingness to acknowledge the extent of the use of force by police, and concerns about civil liability. The cumulative effect of all of those concerns, added to the general problems of conducting a mail survey of law enforcement agencies, made it all the more necessary to work diligently to obtain responses to the questionnaire.

Recognizing these concerns, the letter soliciting the cooperation of the chief executives assured them that, if they completed the questionnaire, their agencies would not be identified by name. Despite these assurances, it is still possible that some agencies refused to participate or provided inaccurate or incomplete information. To the extent that this may have occurred, it must be recognized that the responses analyzed in this study could be biased.

D. OVERALL RELIABILITY AND VALIDITY OF THE RESEARCH

Ultimately, the value of any research depends upon the reliability and validity of its findings. A reliable person is one whose behavior is consistent, dependable, and stable. An unreliable person is one whose behavior is inconsistent, undependable, and unstable. So it is with research.

Reliability is a necessary component of good research. It is not, however, sufficient. It is also necessary that research be valid, that it really measures what it claims to measure. It is quite conceivable, for example, to imagine a measure that produces exactly the same results time after time—one that is highly reliable— but produces the wrong results every time.

To place this report into proper context, it is necessary to assess the overall reliability and validity of the research findings it presents.

There are many different ways of estimating reliability. In one approach, contemporaneous consistency across researchers is examined by having the same measurement instrument used on the same subjects by more than one researcher in order to determine if the results are consistent. A variation of this, applicable to organizations for which there may be many representatives, would be to have the same measurement instrument given to more than one source within the same agency, to see how similar their responses might be. In another approach to the measurement of reliability, that concerned with consistency over time, the same measurement is taken over time by the same researcher, with the aim of determining if the different measurements produce virtually the same results.

With regard to the contemporaneous reliability of this particular research, it would be useful to send the same questionnaire, with different cover letters, to the same agencies, to determine if the responses provided were similar, regardless of who requested the information. Likewise, it would be worthwhile to send the questionnaire to more than one person within the same agencies in order to determine the extent to which their responses resemble each other. Similarly, in order to determine reliability over time, it would be desirable to request the same information for the same period at a later date, in order to determine the extent to which similar results are produced by repeated measurement.

There are also many ways of measuring validity. To determine "face validity," for example, it is only necessary to determine whether the research effort appears, on its face, to be measuring what it is attempting to measure. "Content validity," on the other hand, is measured by examining the content of the measurement effort to determine whether each element measures the concept in question. In another form, "external validity" refers to the extent to which the results of any research are generalizable.

In this study, particular care was taken to improve both the face and content validity of the questionnaire by submitting it to review and pre-testing by scholars and practitioners. In both cases, the validity appears high.

The issue of external validity, however, deserves greater attention. As mentioned in the preceding section, there are many limitations to this research, limitations that can be expected to affect its external validity. First, and most obviously, to the extent that the data for this study were produced by a survey of agencies, to which less than 100 percent responded, it is appropriate to question whether the results can be generalized to agencies that were not included in the sample or did not respond to the survey. Second, even among those agencies that did respond to the survey, many were unable or unwilling to provide certain types of information. To the extent that the data supplied may not represent the agencies that did not supply data, the results cannot be generalized beyond the agencies that provided the data. Third, despite all efforts to avoid it, it is not unlikely that different agencies applied different definitions in responding to the survey. For example, as mentioned above, various agencies may define "filing" or "sustaining" a citizen complaint differently. To the extent that such differences exist, the validity of statements about a common concept is likewise reduced. Fourth, despite assurances of confidentiality, some agencies may have refrained from providing data, or provided data with the intention of presenting a particular impression, leading to biased indicators.

Overriding all of these issues of validity is the basic irremediable fact that most of the information provided in this report, except for that concerning department policies and procedures, comes from official records data. As a result, the report does not purport to deal with the use of force, or complaints of excessive force that go unrecorded. As mentioned throughout this report, such data cannot and should not be interpreted to represent more than what they are intended to be—an official record of an action or transaction maintained and produced at the discretion of a bureaucratic entity. This study has been able to acquire and analyze such data only because the agencies that participated in it have taken it upon themselves to keep and provide records of the use of force by their officers, the nature and disposition of citizen complaints of misconduct by those officers, and the legal consequences of those complaints.

IV. SURVEY RESULTS

This chapter of the report provides a summary of the most important results of the national survey of law enforcement agencies described in the previous section. The first part of the chapter summarizes the information provided by the survey concerning the extent to which law enforcement officers use various types of force. The second part provides data about citizen complaints of excessive force. The third part of the chapter presents survey findings concerning civil suits and criminal charges alleging such excessive force.

The most important findings are presented in figures or tables in the body of the chapter. Other, supportive, tables that are referenced in the report narrative are provided in Appendix B.

A. USE OF FORCE BY POLICE

As mentioned in the review of the literature presented earlier, the use of force is an intrinsic component of the job of a law enforcement officer. A key goal of this study, therefore, was to attempt to determine the extent to which officers actually use various types of force. The types of force about which information was collected included: shots fired at civilians resulting in deaths, woundings, or misses; use of electrical devices (e.g., Tasers, stun guns); use of chemical agents (e.g., Mace, Capstun); use of batons; use of flashlights as force; use of twist locks/wrist locks (i.e., techniques involving twisting the wrist of a suspect); use of bodily force (i.e., use of hands, legs, or other parts of the body); unholstering weapons; use of swarms (I.e., in which several officers surround, immobilize, and handcuff a suspect); use of firm grips; use of neck restraints and/or unconsciousness-rendering holds (e.g., carotid sleeper, choke hold); use of handcuffs or leg restraints; use of come-alongs (i.e., application of a pain-inflicting hold to the hand/wrist to impel suspect movement); dog attacks; and vehicle rammings.

Because the data for this study were collected by means of a survey, any estimates of the extent of the use of force were limited to information provided by the agencies responding to the survey. The reliability and validity of those data are affected by the differing departmental definitions of the various types of force and the differing procedures used by departments to collect and validate this information. Further, interpretation of the estimates must be made with the recognition that, to the extent that the responding agencies may not be representative of law enforcement agencies in general, the estimates themselves may not be representative.

A.1 DEPARTMENT POLICIES REGARDING THE REPORTING OF THE USE OF FORCE

An important obstacle to the creation of accurate estimates of the use of force by police is the fact that law enforcement agencies themselves do not universally and systematically collect information about the use of various types of force. It could be expected that there would be considerable variation in the extent to which various agencies would require that their officers report the use of various types of force. Furthermore, it could also be expected that the reporting of certain types of force, such as shooting a civilian, would more often be required than would others, such as the application of a firm grip.

To provide better insight into the extent to which law enforcement agencies maintain information about the use of force by their officers, the questionnaire requested those agencies to describe their policies regarding the reporting of various types of force. Agencies were requested to indicate whether reporting the use of various types of force or weapons was mandatory, optional, or that there was no policy. Among those departments that answered that reporting was optional, most departments indicated that such reporting was left to the discretion of the individual officer. Telephone interviews with selected departments indicated that some agencies required reporting of certain types of force (e.g., unholstering weapon or use of bodily force) only under particular circumstances, such as when a firearm was pointed at an individual or when the use of bodily force resulted in injury. Agencies indicating that they did not have a policy regarding the reporting of the use of certain types of force or weapons included those that did not have a written policy as well as those that did not allow their officers to use that tactic or weapon (e.g., vehicle ramming, electrical devices, or neck restraints).

In order to understand the extent to which departments could be expected to be able to provide data concerning the use of force by their officers, the remainder of this section summarizes the results of the survey responses concerning the number and percent of agencies that responded that reporting the use of various types of weapons or force was required under all circumstances. Agencies that did not respond to a particular question or said that the specific type of force was not used by personnel in their departments have been excluded from these analyses.

Tables B-1.1 through B-1.5 (in Appendix B) and Figures 3 through 6 provide information concerning the reporting requirements of the responding agencies. In each of those tables, the rows represent the eighteen types of force or weapons about which agencies were asked to provide information. In Table B-1.1, presenting data from all agency types, the columns indicate the type of agency providing the information. These percentages are weighted. Tables B-1.2 through B-1.5 present data provided by sheriffs' departments, county police departments, city police departments, and state agencies, respectively. In those tables, the columns represent agency size, as indicated by the number of sworn personnel in the agency. The number in each cell represents the number of agencies that said that they required their officers to report the use of the type of force represented in that row. In parentheses next to each number is the percentage of the responding agencies of the agency type that required that the use of that type of force be reported.

The final column in the agency-by-size tables for sheriffs' departments, county police departments, and city police departments (Tables B-1.2, B-1.3, and B-1.4) contain percentages weighted by agency size. Figures 3 through 6 also contain weighted percentages.

The variability and levels of reporting requirements must be kept in mind in the ensuing discussions of the incidents of use of force.

Agency Type

Responding to this survey item were 300 sheriffs' departments, 32 county police departments, 721 city police departments, and 45 state agencies. Comparing the percent of each agency type requiring the reporting of force, as shown in Table B-1.1, indicates little variability across agency types in terms of the requirement that shootings be reported. As indicated above, virtually all agencies, regardless of agency type, required that officers report their use of firearms, regardless of whether an injury was produced. For the three firearms-related force categories—denoting civilians shot and killed, shot and wounded, and shot at but not hit—between 92 and 100 percent of the agencies required reporting.

With regard to non-firearms types of force, sheriffs' departments and city police departments were generally more likely than county police departments and state agencies to require reporting. State agencies were fairly consistently the least likely to require reporting. For the most part, however, these differences were small.

Generally, the non-firearms types of force for which reporting was most commonly mandated were vehicle rammings, dog attacks or bites, baton use, use of chemical agents, and use of flashlights as force.

As presented in Figure 3 and Table B-1.1, the results for sheriffs' departments (percentages are weighted) indicate that, in addition to firearms discharges, vehicle rammings were required to be reported by more than 90 percent (91.8%) of the departments. Eighty-two percent (82.4%) required that baton use be reported, 81.1 percent required that flashlights used as force be reported, and 70.2 percent required their officers to report use of chemical agents. Between 50 and 70 percent required that the following be reported: use of neck restraints (69.7%), use of impact devices other than batons or flashlights (68.8%), use of bodily force (66.6%), use of dogs as force (64.6%), and use of electrical devices (53.1%). Less than one-quarter of the sheriffs' departments required the reporting of firm grips (22.4%), use of handcuffs or leg restraints (20.6%), and come-alongs (19.2%).

As indicated in Table B-1.1 and Figure 4, among county police departments 92.4 percent required their officers to report when shots were fired at citizens, even if those shots did not hit the intended targets. Just under ninety percent (89.3%) of county departments required that vehicle rammings be reported. Seventy to ninety percent of such agencies mandated the reporting of dog attacks (82.1%), baton use (80.8%), use of chemical agents (78.5%), and flashlights used as force (72.9%).

Between 50 and 70 percent of county police departments required that their officers report using impact devices other than batons and flashlights (62.1%), bodily force (58.6%) and neck restraints (51.0%). Less than one-quarter mandated the reporting of swarms (20.7%), handcuff and leg restraint use (20.0%), unholstering weapons (15.1%), use of come-alongs (12.9%), and use of firm grips (4.2%).

Among city police departments, over 94 percent required that shots fired be reported. This is presented in B-1.1 and Figure 5. Over 80 percent of city agencies required that vehicle rammings (83.0%), baton use (81.9%), and/or force with flashlights (81.2%) be reported by

Figure 3: Departments Mandating the Reporting of Various Types of Force: Sheriffs' Departments

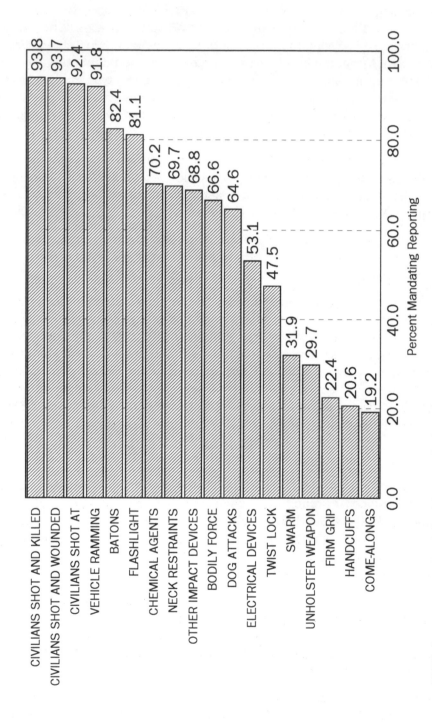

NOTE: Percentages are weighted by agency size.

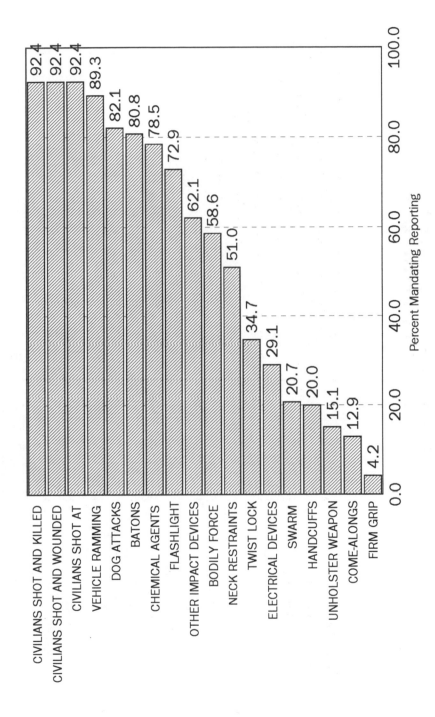

Figure 4 : Departments Mandating the Reporting of Various Types of Force: County Police Departments

CIVILIANS SHOT AND KILLED — 92.4
CIVILIANS SHOT AND WOUNDED — 92.4
CIVILIANS SHOT AT — 92.4
VEHICLE RAMMING — 89.3
DOG ATTACKS — 82.1
BATONS — 80.8
CHEMICAL AGENTS — 78.5
FLASHLIGHT — 72.9
OTHER IMPACT DEVICES — 62.1
BODILY FORCE — 58.6
NECK RESTRAINTS — 51.0
TWIST LOCK — 34.7
ELECTRICAL DEVICES — 29.1
SWARM — 20.7
HANDCUFFS — 20.0
UNHOLSTER WEAPON — 15.1
COME-ALONGS — 12.9
FIRM GRIP — 4.2

Percent Mandating Reporting

NOTE: Percentages are weighted by agency size.

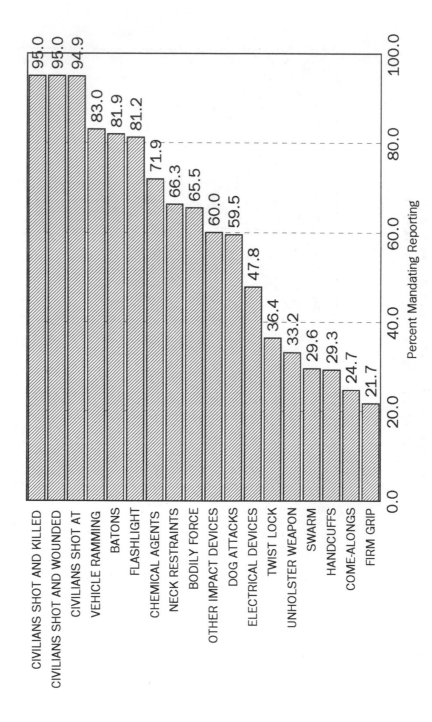

Figure 5 : Departments Mandating the Reporting of Various Types of Force: City Police Departments

CIVILIANS SHOT AND KILLED — 95.0
CIVILIANS SHOT AND WOUNDED — 95.0
CIVILIANS SHOT AT — 94.9
VEHICLE RAMMING — 83.0
BATONS — 81.9
FLASHLIGHT — 81.2
CHEMICAL AGENTS — 71.9
NECK RESTRAINTS — 66.3
BODILY FORCE — 65.5
OTHER IMPACT DEVICES — 60.0
DOG ATTACKS — 59.5
ELECTRICAL DEVICES — 47.8
TWIST LOCK — 36.4
UNHOLSTER WEAPON — 33.2
SWARM — 29.6
HANDCUFFS — 29.3
COME-ALONGS — 24.7
FIRM GRIP — 21.7

Percent Mandating Reporting

0.0   20.0   40.0   60.0   80.0   100.0

NOTE: Percentages are weighted by agency size.

their officers. One-half to three-fourths required the reporting of the use of chemical agents (71.9%), neck restraints (66.3%), bodily force (65.5%), impact devices other than batons or flashlights (60.0%), and/or dog bites (59.5%). Less than one-quarter required that the use of come-alongs (24.7%) or firm grips (21.7%) be reported.

One hundred percent of the state agencies required that officers report all shots fired at citizens and 90.5 percent mandated the reporting of vehicle rammings. Between one-half and three-fourths of the state agencies required the reporting of use of flashlights as force (70.5%), dog bites or attacks (69.2%), the use of batons (68.2%), use of chemical agents (66.7%), use of neck restraints (60.0%), and use of bodily force (56.1%). These results are contained in B-1.1 and Figure 6.

AGENCY SIZE

Tables B.1-2 through B.1-5 provide the results for each of the four types of agencies by seven categories of agency size, based on the number of sworn personnel in each agency. As explained above, we will not attempt to draw any conclusions regarding the variations among size categories of either county police departments or state agencies, due to the small cell sizes. These data, however, are contained in Tables B.1-3 and B.1-5. As seen in Table B.1-2, all but one of the sheriffs' agencies that did not require the reporting of shots fired (whether or not they hit a citizen) were in the smallest size category, having between 1 and 24 sworn personnel. Similarly, larger agencies were more likely to require the reporting of dog attacks. On the other hand, larger agencies were less likely to mandate the reporting of the unholstering of weapons.

Table B-1.4 indicates that all of the city police departments that did not require the reporting of shootings that resulted in the killing or wounding of a civilian had fewer than 50 sworn personnel. Likewise, larger departments were more likely than smaller ones to require reporting of the use of electrical devices, chemical agents, impact devices other than batons or flashlights, neck restraints, dog attacks, and vehicle rammings. Conversely, as with sheriffs' departments, more of the smaller departments required that their officers report weapon unholsterings.

A.2 AGENCIES PROVIDING RESPONSES CONCERNING USE OF VARIOUS TYPES OF FORCE

Although each agency was requested to provide information about the number of incidents in which various types of force were used in 1991, the previous section demonstrates that there is considerable variability with respect to the extent to which officers are required to report their use of such force. As a result, it can be expected that there would likewise be a great deal of variability in terms of the ability of agencies to provide information concerning the use of force.

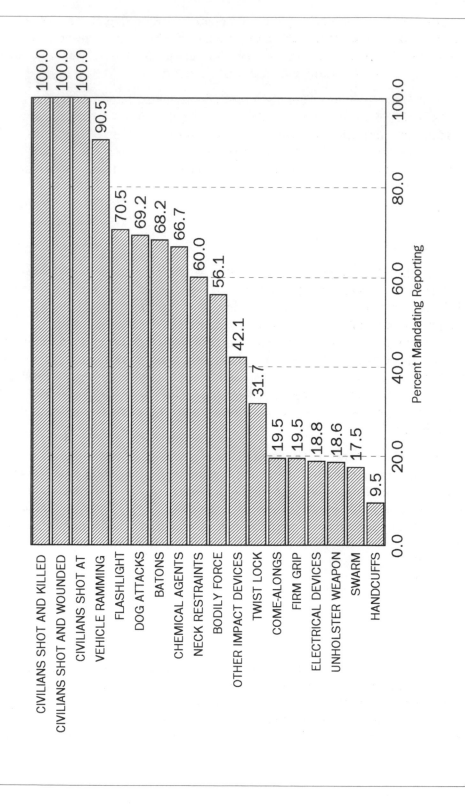

Figure 6 : Departments Mandating the Reporting of Various Types of Force: State Agencies

To provide some insight into the extent to which differential reporting occurred, Tables B-2.1 through B-2.5 indicate the number of departments that provided data in the survey on the number of force incidents that occurred in 1991 within various force type categories. The percentage of agencies providing these data are indicated in parentheses following the number. (Because these percentages are provided as an indicator of the response rate for this particular set of measures among the sample of responding agencies, they have not been weighted according to the agency size distribution of the universe from which the sample was selected.) Information concerning these response rates—which are relevant to the reliability and validity of the force data—should be borne in mind when interpreting the data in subsequent sections regarding the frequency and rate at which force was reported to have been used by officers.

AGENCY TYPE

The percentages of sheriffs' departments, county police departments, and city police departments that provided data in each of the force categories were generally quite similar. In contrast, state agencies were least likely to provide data concerning incidents of each type of force.

AGENCY SIZE

Tables B-2.2 through B-2.5 provide information, for each agency type, concerning the number and percentage of agencies that provided data concerning the number of reported incidents of various types of use of force in 1991. As indicated in Table B-2.2, there was some tendency for the larger sheriffs' departments to be less likely to provide data than smaller agencies.

Table B-2.3 reveals that, among county police departments, the rate at which information was provided did not vary consistently by agency size.

As shown in Table B-2.4, larger city police departments were generally less likely than small ones to have provided use of force incident data.

The force data did not appear to be differentially provided by state agencies of different sizes. This can be seen in Table B-2.5.

A.3 NUMBER OF REPORTED INCIDENTS OF THE USE OF FORCE IN 1991

Tables B-3.1 through B-3.5 provide the data submitted by responding agencies concerning the number of incidents involving the various categories of force that occurred in 1991. The numbers in parentheses in those tables indicate for each cell the number of agencies that provided these data. Because these data were provided by varying numbers of agencies with widely divergent numbers of sworn personnel, this information should be used only to provide a basis for interpreting the information presented in the next section, which is rates of incidents per 1,000 sworn officers. These numbers are unweighted.

AGENCY TYPE

As shown by Table B-3.1, among sheriffs' departments, the use of handcuffs was the most frequently mentioned type of force used; a total of 1,817 such incidents were reported to have occurred in 49 departments during 1991. The use of bodily force was the second most commonly reported type of force; 1,581 such incidents were reported by 81 agencies. The third most frequently mentioned type of force was the use of "come-along" tactics; 837 such incidents were reported by 70 agencies. There were 394 reports of the use of firm grips, 273 reports of unholstering weapons, 265 reported dog attacks, 242 uses of chemical agents, and 230 reports of the use of a baton. No other type of force was reported more than 200 times.

Table B-3.1 also presents the results among county police departments. As that table indicates, the most commonly reported type of force among those departments was the use of bodily force; 288 such incidents were reported by 12 agencies. The use of handcuffs was reported in 209 incidents, followed by 144 dog attacks, and 133 incidents of the use of chemical agents. No other type of force was reported to have been used as many as 100 times.

Use of bodily force was the most commonly reported type of force among city police departments; a total of 4,425 such incidents were reported by 198 agencies to have occurred in 1991, followed by 3,487 uses of chemical agents, and 3,295 incidents involving handcuffs or leg restraints. The use of batons was reported in 1,061 cases; the use of "come-along" techniques was reported in 1,057 cases. Agencies reported 969 incidents in which officers unholstered their weapons, 880 dog attacks, 761 cases of using a twist lock, 569 uses of electrical devices, and 503 uses of a firm grip. No other type of force was reported to have been used as many as 500 times.

Among state agencies, bodily force was reportedly used by 12 agencies in 2,203 incidents, by far the most frequently mentioned type of force used. In addition, there were 76 reports of the use of chemical agents, 71 cases in which officers unholstered their weapons, and 68 cases in which vehicles were rammed. No other type of force was reported to have been used as many as 45 times.

AGENCY SIZE

Although, as pointed out above, meaningful comparisons of these data require standardization by agency size, it is worth noting that, among sheriffs' departments, as shown in Table B-3.2, the overwhelming majority of incidents concerning shootings were reported by agencies with more than 1,000 sworn personnel. It is also noteworthy, however, that those large agencies reported far less than half of the incidents of any other type of force.

Overall, as shown in Table B-3.3, the majority of reported incidents came from county police departments with between 100 and 499 sworn officers, those that constituted a majority of the reporting agencies. A large number of shootings, however, were reported by agencies with more than 500 sworn personnel.

Table B-3.4 indicates that city police departments with 1,000 or more sworn personnel reported the most incidents of use of force in 10 of 18 categories. Since this category includes agencies with extremely large numbers of officers, this finding is not as notable as the fact that agencies with fewer officers reported more incidents in the remaining 8 categories. (Though in all of those eight categories seven or fewer of the largest agencies provided data.)

In general, as shown in Table B-3.5, state agencies with 1,000 or more sworn officers provided a majority of the reports of use of force.

A.4 REPORTED INCIDENTS OF THE USE OF FORCE PER 1,000 SWORN OFFICERS

In order to standardize the absolute number of reported incidents of the use of force, a new indicator was created representing the number of such incidents reported for every 1,000 sworn personnel. This measure was calculated by dividing the total number of incidents reported for each type of force by any particular group and dividing by the number of sworn officers in that group. The result was then multiplied by 1,000. Table 6.1 presents the weighted rates for the reported use in 1991 of each type of force for each agency type. In parentheses are the numbers of agencies providing the data upon which the rates were calculated. Figures 7 through 10 provide graphic representations of the rates for each force type for each of the four agency types. For each agency type, the categories of force are presented in order of response rate. It is important to keep in mind, when interpreting these rates, the number of agencies providing data for each category.

AGENCY TYPE

As shown in Table 6.1 and Figure 7, handcuffs use, weapon unholsterings, bodily force, and come-alongs were the most frequently reported types of force used among sheriffs' departments. They were reportedly used in 1991 at rates of 195.1, 193.4, 177.0, and 113.3 per 1,000 sworn officers, respectively. It is important to keep in mind that these weighted rates were based on information provided by a limited number of departments and that only a limited number of departments require reporting of these types of force. For instance, the rate for handcuffs use should be interpreted in view of the fact that 79.4 percent of sheriffs' departments, weighted based on agency size, did not require their officers to report the use of handcuffs, coupled with the fact that 82.5 percent of the responding departments did not provide data concerning the number of incidents of this particular type of force. Similarly, the reporting of the unholstering of weapons was required by 29.7 percent of the agencies, and 22.8 percent of the agencies provided data. Providing data on bodily force and come-alongs were 26.7 percent and 23.1 percent of the agencies, respectively.

Table 6.1

Reported Incidents of Police Use of Force Per 1,000 Sworn Officers:
By Agency Type

Type of Force	Agency Type			
	Sheriffs' Departments	County Police Departments	City Police Departments	State Agencies
Civilians shot and killed	0.2	0.8	0.9	0.4
Civilians shot and wounded but not killed	0.2	1.6	0.2	0.4
Civilians shot at but not hit	8.1	5.8	3.0	1.8
Electrical devices (e.g., Taser)	10.3	13.3	5.4	0.4
Chemical agents (e.g., Mace, Capstun)	49.3	22.3	36.2	6.9
Batons	12.8	16.6	36.0	2.8
Other impact devices (e.g., saps, soft projectiles, rubber bullets)	0.3	0.3	2.4	1.5
Flashlight	4.8	11.6	21.7	0.7
Twist lock/wrist lock	11.8	1.8	80.9	4.2
Bodily force (e.g., arm, foot, leg, etc.)	177.0	164.7	272.2	200.5
Unholstering weapon	193.4	19.3	129.9	9.9
Swarm	19.1	2.5	126.7	0.0
Firm Grip	19.6	4.3	57.7	0.0
Neck restraints/unconsciousness rendering holds	1.1	0.2	1.4	0.9
Handcuff/leg restraint	195.1	73.9	490.4	7.7
Come-alongs	113.3	0.9	226.8	1.5
Dog attacks or bites	18.3	15.4	6.5	2.6
Vehicle ramming	4.7	0.1	1.0	3.7

NOTE: Rates are weighted

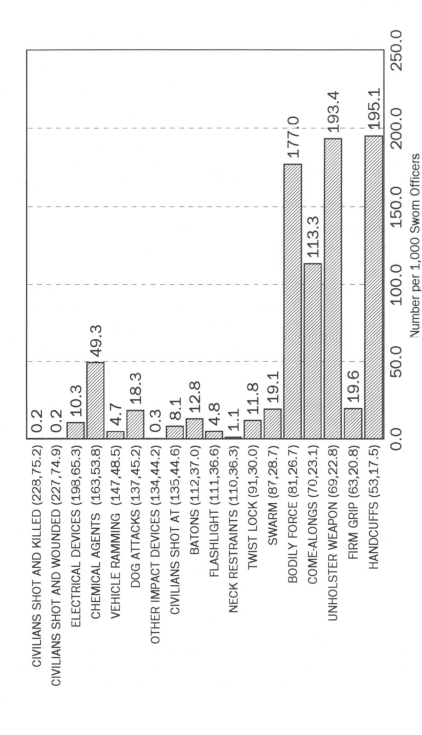

Figure 7: Reported 1991 Incidents of the Use of Force per 1,000 Sworn Officers: Sheriffs' Departments

CIVILIANS SHOT AND KILLED (228,75.2)	0.2
CIVILIANS SHOT AND WOUNDED (227,74.9)	0.2
ELECTRICAL DEVICES (198,65.3)	10.3
CHEMICAL AGENTS (163,53.8)	49.3
VEHICLE RAMMING (147,48.5)	4.7
DOG ATTACKS (137,45.2)	18.3
OTHER IMPACT DEVICES (134,44.2)	0.3
CIVILIANS SHOT AT (135,44.6)	8.1
BATONS (112,37.0)	12.8
FLASHLIGHT (111,36.6)	4.8
NECK RESTRAINTS (110,36.3)	1.1
TWIST LOCK (91,30.0)	11.8
SWARM (87,28.7)	19.1
BODILY FORCE (81,26.7)	177.0
COME-ALONGS (70,23.1)	113.3
UNHOLSTER WEAPON (69,22.8)	193.4
FIRM GRIP (63,20.8)	19.6
HANDCUFFS (53,17.5)	195.1

Number per 1,000 Sworn Officers

NOTE: Rates are weighted by agency size. Figures in parentheses represent the number and percentage of agencies providing responses.

Next most frequently used by sheriffs' departments, but at a much lower rate, were chemical agents, reportedly used 49.3 times in 1991 per 1,000 sworn officers. Data regarding this type of force were provided by 53.8 percent of the agencies.

Rates of between 10 and 20 incidents per 1,000 sworn officers were reported by sheriffs' departments for firm grips (19.6), swarms (19.1), dog bites/attacks (18.3), baton use (12.8), twist locks/wrist locks (11.8), and use of electrical devices (10.3). The percentage of agencies providing data varied from 20.8 for firm grip to 65.3 for electrical devices.

All of these rates must be interpreted in view of the variable reporting requirements of the responding sheriffs' agencies, which ranged from a high of over 93 percent for shootings that resulted in wounds or death, to a low of 19.2 percent for come-alongs. In addition, it should be noted that the rate at which responding sheriffs' departments provided data on the questionnaire ranged from 75.2 percent for shootings that resulted in death to 17.5 percent for use of handcuffs and/or leg restraints.

Table 6.1 and Figure 8 provide information concerning the rates of force reported among county police departments. Again, in this figure, the categories of force are presented in descending order of response rate.

Responding county police departments indicated that the use of bodily force in 1991 was reported at a rate of 164.7 per 1,000 sworn officers, the highest rate among the types of force examined. As noted earlier, 58.6 percent of responding agencies indicated that their officers were required to report the use of bodily force; 37.5 percent of responding agencies provided data concerning incidents of the use of bodily force on the questionnaire.

The use of handcuffs/leg restraints by officers of county police departments was reported at a rate of 73.9 times per 1,000 sworn officers in 1991. This rate was second only to that for bodily force. Interpretation of this rate should include recognizing that 80.0 percent of responding agencies indicated that they did not require their officers to report incidents of handcuffing, and that 75.0 percent of the responding agencies did not provide data concerning the use of handcuffs by their officers.

Dropping considerably, the next highest rates reported by county police departments were for use of chemical agents, unholstering weapons, use of batons, and dog attacks or bites. In order, these rates are 22.3, 19.3, 16.6, and 15.4. Reporting each of these actions was required by between 15.1 and 82.1 percent of responding agencies, and of the agencies completing the questionnaire, between 21.9 percent and 56.3 percent provided data concerning the number of 1991 incidents of each type of force.

The lowest rates of force were reported for come-alongs, civilians shot and killed, the use of impact devices other than batons and flashlights, neck restraints, and vehicle rammings. These rates were 0.9, 0.8, 0.3, 0.2, and 0.1. Between 12.9 and 92.4 percent of responding agencies indicated that they required their officers to report the use of these types of force; between 31.3 and 81.3 percent of responding agencies provided data about these types of incidents.

Figure 8: Reported 1991 Incidents of the Use of Force per 1,000 Sworn Officers: County Police Departments

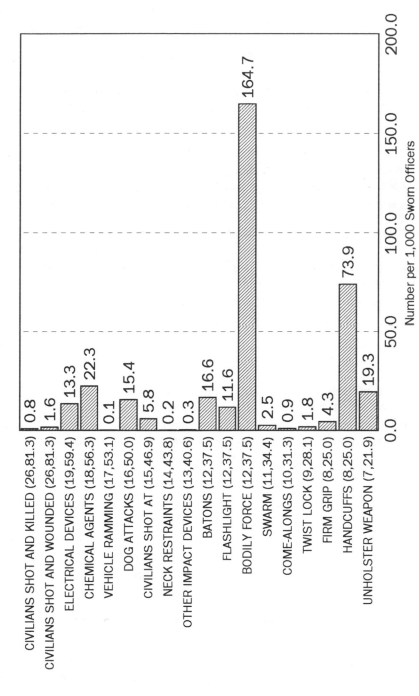

NOTE: Rates are weighted by agency size. Figures in parentheses represent the number and percentage of agencies providing responses.

Figure 9 and Table 6.1 provide information about the reported rates of various types of force among city police departments. The use of handcuffs had the highest reported rate of use in 1991, 490.4 per 1,000 sworn officers. To put this rate in perspective, it should be recalled that 70.7 percent of the agencies did not require the reporting of the use of handcuffs, and 79.3 percent did not provide information about their use on the questionnaire.

Bodily force was reported to have been used at a rate of 272.1 times per 1,000 sworn officers among city police departments, the second highest rate. It should be kept in mind that 36.7 percent of the responding city agencies did not require their officers to report the use of bodily force, and 72.9 percent of the agencies responding to the survey did not provide information concerning the use of such force.

High rates of force use were also reported for come-alongs (226.6 per 1,000 sworn officers), weapon unholsterings (129.9 per 1,000), and swarms (126.7 per 1,000). For these types of force between 24.7 percent and 33.2 percent of departments mandate their reporting and between 22.4 percent and 26.1 percent of the agencies provided data.

Rates of use ranging from 20 to 90 incidents per 1,000 officers were reported for twist lock/wrist lock (80.9), firm grips (57.7) use of chemical agents (36.2), use of batons (36.0), and use of flashlights as force (21.7). The percent of departments that required the reporting of these types of force ranged from 21.7 percent for firm grip, to 81.9 percent for use of batons. The departments providing incident data ranged from 20.9 percent for data concerning the use of firm grips to 51.4 percent for the use of chemical agents.

No other type of force was reported to have been used at rates higher than 7 per 1,000 sworn officers.

The rates of reported incidents of force among state agencies are presented in Figure 10 as well as Table 6.1. The results indicate that bodily force had the highest rate of reported use in 1991, 200.5 per 1,000 sworn officers. It should be recalled that the reporting of the use of bodily force by their officers was required by 56.1 percent of the responding state agencies and that 26.7 of the agencies provided data on the number of incidents of the use of this type of force.

None of the other rates exceeded 10 per 1,000 sworn officers, including unholstering weapons (9.9 per 1,000), handcuffing (7.7 per 1,000), use of chemical agents (6.9 per 1,000), and twist locks (4.2 per 1,000). The percent of agencies requiring the reporting of the use of those types of force varied from a high of 66.7 percent for chemical agents to a low of 9.5 percent for the use of handcuffs. The number of agencies providing data on the use of these types of force ranged from 31.1 percent for chemical agents to 13.3 percent for handcuffs.

No other type of force was reported by state agencies to have been used at rates higher than 4.0 per 1,000 sworn officers.

The relatively low reported rates of use of all types of force (except bodily force) in general, and of handcuffs in particular seems to reflect the fact that the role of officers in state agencies is less likely than those in other agencies to require taking suspects into custody.

Figure 9: Reported 1991 Incidents of the Use of Force per 1,000 Sworn Officers: City Police Departments

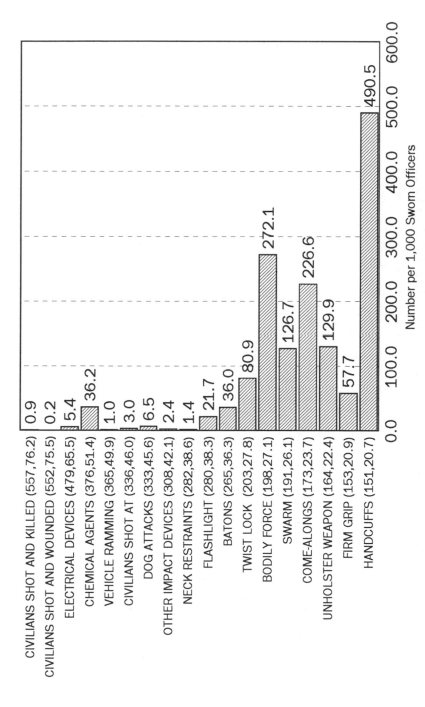

NOTE: Rates are weighted by agency size. Figures in parentheses represent the number and percentage of agencies providing responses.

Figure 10: Reported 1991 Incidents of the Use of Force per 1,000 Sworn Officers: State Agencies

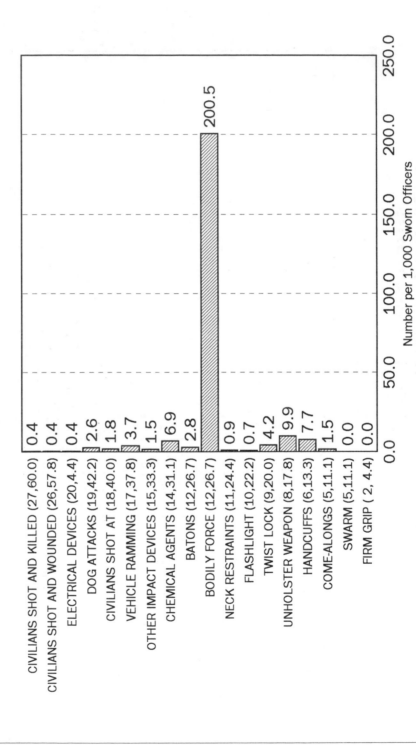

NOTE: Figures in parentheses represent the number and percentage of agencies providing responses.

AGENCY SIZE

Tables 6.2 and 6.3 present the results for sheriffs' departments and city police departments by agency size. Because of the small number of sheriffs' departments in the top three size categories, these largest agencies have been grouped together in Table 6.2. (Table B-4.1 contains the information for the original seven size categories.) As indicated in Table 6.2, there was no consistent tendency, across types of force, for sheriffs' agencies of one size to differ from others. Larger agencies did, however, indicate notably higher rates of shootings that resulted in injury or death. On the other hand, smaller agencies tended to report higher rates of vehicle rammings, use of chemical agents, swarms and unholstering of weapons.

As seen in Table 6.3, city agencies with more than 50 sworn officers consistently had higher rates at which citizens were shot and killed or wounded and higher rates of dog attacks than did smaller agencies. On the other hand, smaller agencies had generally higher rates of use of flashlights, bodily force, firm grips, and handcuffs, as well as higher reported rates at which weapons were unholstered. The smallest agencies, those with fewer than 25 officers, reported the highest rates of use for several force categories.

The results by agency size for county police departments and state agencies are contained in Tables B-4.2 and B-4.3.

A.5 FACTORS ASSOCIATED WITH THE USE OF FORCE

As indicated in the review of the literature presented previously, a number of factors have been identified that could conceivably affect the rate at which officers use force. This section provides the results of the national survey pertaining to those factors.

A.5.1 SELECTION PROCEDURES

Departments were asked to indicate whether or not they required psychological or psychiatric evaluations of pre-service officers as part of their selection procedures. The responses are contained in Tables B-5.1 through B-5.5. The percentages in Table B-5.1 are weighted.

AGENCY TYPE

The weighted percentages indicate that proportionately fewer sheriffs' departments mandated this type of evaluation relative to the other types of agencies. Less than sixty percent (58.3%) of the sheriffs' departments mandated this type of evaluation, compared to 68.8 percent of the city police departments, 75.6 percent of the county police departments, and 86.7 percent of the state agencies.

Table 6.2

Reported Incidents of Police Use of Force Per 1,000 Sworn Officers: Sheriffs' Departments by Agency Size

Type of Force	Number of Sworn Personnel						Weighted Row Rate
	1-24	25-49	50-99	100-249	250 or more	
Civilians shot and killed	0.0 (36)	0.8 (34)	0.0 (59)	0.6 (61)	1.3 (38)	0.2
Civilians shot and wounded but not killed	0.0 (36)	0.0 (34)	1.5 (59)	0.9 (61)	2.1 (33)	0.2
Civilians shot at but not hit	11.8 (19)	1.9 (16)	0.4 (38)	1.3 (41)	2.8 (21)	8.1
Electrical devices (e.g., Taser)	15.5 (35)	0.0 (30)	0.6 (50)	4.8 (52)	1.0 (31)	10.3
Chemical agents (e.g., Mace, Capstun)	45.2 (32)	107.8 (23)	17.2 (42)	4.7 (39)	4.1 (27)	49.3
Batons	12.4 (23)	4.3 (20)	13.2 (27)	45.4 (26)	2.5 (16)	12.8
Other impact devices (e.g., saps, soft projectiles)	0.0 (26)	1.3 (22)	0.0 (32)	0.7 (35)	1.9 (15)	0.3
Flashlight	3.2 (23)	10.1 (20)	2.3 (25)	12.4 (28)	1.3 (15)	4.8
Twist lock/wrist lock	11.2 (18)	13.8 (19)	17.4 (21)	7.2 (21)	5.8 (12)	11.8
Bodily force (e.g., arm, foot, leg, etc.)	220.0 (18)	75.0 (17)	62.0 (17)	216.9 (17)	111.0 (12)	177.0
Unholstering weapon	283.2 (12)	18.7 (17)	43.8 (16)	61.2 (17)	4.8 (7)	193.4
Swarm	28.3 (17)	4.7 (18)	0.0 (18)	1.9 (25)	0.3 (9)	19.1
Firm grip	3.5 (12)	16.5 (13)	118.1 (16)	44.5 (15)	18.8 (7)	19.6
Neck restraints/unconsciousness-rendering holds	0.0 (24)	5.8 (20)	0.0 (30)	1.4 (23)	0.0 (13)	1.1
Handcuff/leg restraint	127.7 (6)	48.1 (12)	963.9 (13)	51.9 (11)	315.1 (7)	195.1
Come-alongs	162.0 (13)	1.9 (16)	13.4 (17)	9.6 (15)	218.0 (9)	113.3
Dog attacks or bites	22.7 (24)	8.3 (21)	15.2 (38)	5.2 (36)	17.0 (18)	18.3
Vehicle ramming	5.2 (27)	4.9 (24)	4.4 (36)	1.7 (42)	0.3 (18)	4.7

Note: Numbers in Parentheses represent responding Agencies

Table 6.3

Reported Incidents of Police Use of Force Per 1,000 Sworn Officers: City Police Departments by Agency Size

Type of Force	Number of Sworn Personnel					Weighted Row Rate
	1-24	25-49	50-99	100-249	250 or more	
Civilians shot and killed	0.9 (99)	0.3 (83)	1.3 (132)	1.4 (158)	1.3 (85)	0.9
Civilians shot and wounded but not killed	0.0 (99)	0.3 (83)	1.3 (132)	1.2 (157)	2.5 (81)	0.2
Civilians shot at but not hit	3.4 (54)	1.2 (44)	0.6 (86)	2.0 (99)	3.6 (53)	3.0
Electrical devices (e.g., Taser)	5.8 (96)	0.4 (74)	14.0 (117)	3.1 (130)	4.9 (62)	5.4
Chemical agents (e.g., Mace, Capstun)	32.8 (87)	66.3 (63)	20.3 (86)	24.9 (90)	41.8 (50)	36.2
Batons	39.7 (71)	21.5 (47)	18.3 (61)	28.8 (58)	28.0 (28)	36.0
Other impact devices (e.g., saps, soft projectiles)	2.4 (75)	1.4 (59)	0.2 (71)	8.4 (73)	3.9 (30)	2.4
Flashlight	26.1 (72)	5.5 (51)	3.3 (66)	6.8 (67)	2.5 (24)	21.7
Twist lock/wrist lock	98.9 (60)	9.8 (37)	18.3 (43)	13.8 (43)	26.0 (20)	80.9
Bodily force (e.g., arm, foot, leg, etc.)	203.5 (55)	820.7 (32)	150.9 (44)	99.5 (45)	106.3 (22)	272.1
Unholstering weapon	148.6 (51)	69.3 (30)	53.5 (36)	37.7 (34)	38.5 (13)	129.9
Swarm	159.7 (65)	0.8 (34)	4.2 (38)	0.2 (37)	21.2 (17)	126.7
Firm grip	66.0 (49)	21.8 (29)	48.5 (32)	11.3 (29)	20.8 (14)	57.7
Neck restraints/unconsciousness-rendering holds	0.0 (68)	1.1 (50)	19.7 (63)	11.4 (67)	3.7 (34)	1.4
Handcuff/leg restraint	422.2 (38)	1,026.0 (24)	614.2 (37)	94.3 (34)	8.2 (13)	490.4
Come-alongs	268.3 (56)	25.8 (28)	239.6 (37)	2.5 (35)	12.6 (17)	226.6
Dog attacks or bites	4.7 (74)	5.6 (63)	21.4 (72)	31.2 (84)	13.2 (40)	6.5
Vehicle ramming	1.1 (81)	0.0 (67)	1.1 (85)	1.0 (96)	0.2 (38)	1.0

Note: Numbers in Parentheses Represent Responding Agencies

AGENCY SIZE

Tables B-5.2 through B-5.5 provide the results for each type of agency by agency size. As seen in Table B-5.2, among sheriffs' departments, there was a positive relationship between agency size and the use of psychological or psychiatric exams for pre-service personnel. Approximately half (51.2%) of the smallest sheriffs' agencies, with 1 to 24 sworn personnel, required these evaluations, compared to 100.0 percent of the agencies with 500 or more sworn personnel.

The lowest percentage of city agencies requiring psychological evaluations was among those with fewer than 25 sworn personnel; in that category, 62.8 percent required such examinations. Among city agencies with between 25 and 49 officers, 89.1 percent had such a requirement. Approximately 95 percent of agencies with more than 50 sworn personnel required such evaluations.

A.5.2   TRAINING

Responding agencies provided various types of information regarding their recruit training. In particular, agencies were asked to indicate the length in hours of their academy training, whether or not they had formal Field Training Officer programs, and the number of months that recruits were on probation following academy training. In addition, agencies were asked to provide information concerning the frequency at which their officers were required to requalify with their service weapons.

A.5.2A LENGTH IN HOURS OF ACADEMY TRAINING

Tables B-6.1 and B-6.2 present information provided by responding departments concerning the number of hours of academy training. Table B-6.1 contains, for each agency type, the weighted average number of academy hours. Table B-6.2 presents the results for each agency type by size.

AGENCY TYPE

As indicated in Table B-6.1, state agencies had the highest average number of academy training hours. The average for state agencies was 789.3 hours, compared to 608.3 for county police departments, 468.0 for city police departments, and 395.4 for sheriffs' departments.

AGENCY SIZE

Among both sheriffs and municipal departments, as shown in Table B-6.2, there was a positive relationship between agency size and the average number of hours spent in academy training. For instance, sheriffs' departments with 1 to 24 sworn personnel required an average of 333.5 hours, compared to over 600 hours in agencies with 250 or more sworn personnel.

Similarly, the average length of the academy training among city agencies with 250 or more sworn personnel (over 700 hours) was 160 percent of the corresponding average (448.2) of the departments with 1 to 24 sworn personnel.

A.5.2B THE EXISTENCE OF A FORMAL FIELD TRAINING OFFICER PROGRAM

Departments were asked whether or not they provided formalized Field Training Officer (FTO) programs. The results from this survey item are presented, by agency type, in Table B-7.1. In addition, results are presented for each agency by agency size in Tables B-7.2 through B-7.5.

AGENCY TYPE

When the survey results for sheriffs' departments, county police departments, and city police departments arc weighted to reflect the actual distribution of agency sizes in the nation, more state agencies and county police departments than the other two types of agencies provided formalized FTO programs for recruits. Over 93 percent (93.3%) of the state agencies and 75.6 percent of the county police departments provided FTO training, compared to 52.1 percent of the city police departments, and 43.9 percent of the sheriffs' departments.

AGENCY SIZE

Among sheriffs' departments and city police departments, there was a tendency for larger agencies to be more likely to have formal FTO programs than smaller agencies.

A.5.2C AVERAGE LENGTH OF PROBATION PERIODS

Tables B-8.1 and B-8.2 provide information concerning the average length, in months, of probation periods for recruits. Table B-8.1 presents weighted averages.

AGENCY TYPE

The average length of probation periods were fairly similar across agencies types. The average length of probation periods was 12.8 months among state agencies, 11.7 months among county police departments, 10.3 months among city police departments, and 8.9 among sheriffs' departments.

AGENCY SIZE

As indicated in Table B-8.2, larger sheriffs' agencies tended to have longer probation periods than smaller ones. For instance, among sheriffs' departments, the smallest agencies averaged 8.1 months of probation compared to an average of 12.3 months among the largest agencies (with 500 or more sworn personnel).

There was no clear relationship between average length of probation periods and agency size among city police departments. The longest such periods were found among agencies with between 50 and 249 sworn personnel.

A.5.2D OVERALL RECRUIT TRAINING

Table 7 provides the results for each agency type for the three aspects of recruit training. State agencies have the longest averages for both length of academy training and length of probation. Additionally, a larger proportion of state agencies, compared to the other three types of agencies, have formal FTO programs. In contrast, sheriffs' departments have, on average, the shortest academies and the shortest probationary periods. Additionally, they have the smallest proportion of departments with FTO programs.

A.5.2E FREQUENCY OF REQUALIFICATION WITH SERVICE WEAPONS

The questionnaire also inquired about the frequency of required requalification with service weapons of in-service personnel. The results of this inquiry, using categories of once per year or less, twice per year, or more than twice per year, are contained in Tables B-9.1 through B-9.5.

AGENCY TYPE

When weighted percentages are considered, more sheriffs' departments and city police departments than the other two categories of agencies required less than two requalifications per year. Forty-one percent (41.0%) of the sheriffs' departments and 38.0 percent of the city police departments required one or fewer requalifications per year, compared to 29.1 percent of the county police departments and 27.3 percent of the state agencies.

Within both county police departments and state agencies, pluralities of agencies required two requalifications per year. That is, 42.7 percent of the county police departments and 38.6 percent of the state agencies required two requalifications.

Table 7

Average Number of Academy Training Hours, Percentage with Formal Field Training Officer Program, Average Number of Months of Probation Required for Recruits: By Agency Type

Training Indicator	Agency Type			
	Sheriffs' Departments	County Police Departments	City Police Departments	State Agencies
Average Number of Academy Training Hours	395.4	608.3	468.0	789.3
Percentage with Formal Field Training Officer Program	43.9	75.6	52.1	93.3
Average Number of Months of Probation Required for Recruits	8.9	11.7	10.3	12.8

NOTE: Averages and percentages are weighted by agency size

AGENCY SIZE

As indicated in Tables B-9.2, the smallest sheriffs' departments (those with 1 to 24 sworn personnel) were most likely to require fewer than two requalifications per year.

As indicated in Table B-9.4, there was no clear relationship among city police departments between agency size and requalification requirements.

A.5.3 MONITORING

As discussed earlier, some agencies have adopted policies that require officers to report some, or all, uses of force. The questionnaire went on to ask whether agencies used these reports to monitor the use of force by their officers. In particular, agencies were asked to indicate whether, regardless of whether or not citizen complaints or civil suits were filed, they a) reviewed all use of force reports, b) reviewed selected reports, or c) did not review any use of force reports. The results of the analyses of these responses are contained in Tables B-10.1 through B-10.5.

AGENCY TYPE

A majority of the agencies within each agency type indicated that they reviewed all reports of force. Using weighted percentages, reviewing all reports were 55.8 percent of the state agencies, 65.3 percent of the city police departments, 70.0 percent of the sheriffs' agencies, and 72.6 percent of the county police departments. Agencies that reviewed selected reports included 14.8 percent of the county police departments, 16.4 percent of the sheriffs' departments, 22.9 percent of the city police departments, and 30.2 percent of the state agencies. Between 11.8 percent and 14.0 percent of the agencies in each type conducted no review.

AGENCY SIZE

There was no apparent relationship between sheriffs' department size and the extent to which those agencies said they reviewed all or selected force reports. A majority of agencies in each size category (with the two top size categories combined to achieve adequate cell size) indicated that all reports of force were reviewed.

Similarly, there was no relationship among city police departments between force report review practices and agency size.

B. CITIZEN COMPLAINTS OF EXCESSIVE FORCE

As indicated in the review of the literature, the primary method by which citizens can register their concerns about the use of excessive force by police officers is by means of the citizen complaint process. To provide a better understanding of that process, agencies were requested to indicate, by complaint type, how many complaints citizens filed against their officers in 1991 and the dispositions of those complaints. Departments were requested to exclude complaints that resulted from interactions between officers and citizens in jail settings. This section presents the results of the analyses of citizen complaints of excessive, undue, or unnecessary use of force. These analyses will be presented in terms of the reported number of complaints received and, in order to provide standardized estimates, the number of complaints received per 1,000 sworn officers. Each of these sets of data are presented by agency type and by agency type and size. In addition, this section provides comparisons between the demographic characteristics of complainants and the general population, as well as between the demographic characteristics of officers receiving complaints and those of officers in general.

The reliability and validity of these complaint data are affected by the many different ways departments categorize complaints of misconduct. These variations became apparent during the development of the instrument as a result of reviews of departmental documentation and discussions with police personnel. Fortunately, the most consistent categorization of misconduct complaints among departments was with regard to excessive use of force. Nevertheless, the Police Foundation questionnaire attempted to encompass the breadth of definitions used by departments by labeling this category "excessive/undue/unnecessary use of force; brutality (including use of weapons, cuffs, etc." However, this problem of categorizing complaints should be kept in mind when interpreting the results.

Procedures used by departments to count complaints of misconduct may also vary and thus affect the reliability and validity of these data. Although departments were requested to indicate the "total number of citizens' complaints filed against employees," the definition of "filing" may vary across agencies. In some, any complaint, whether written or oral, submitted anonymously or by an identified person, certified or not, may be counted as "filed." In others, there may be certain requirements that must be met (e.g., submission in writing, certification) before a complaint is considered "filed." Some departments may count those complaints that were filed but subsequently were withdrawn by the complainants; others may exclude withdrawn complaints.

Another limitation to these data, as explained more fully below, is that approximately 25 percent of the agencies that returned surveys did not provide the requested complaint data. Thus, the interpretation of these estimates must be made with the recognition that, to the extent that the responding agencies may not be representative of law enforcement agencies in general, the estimates themselves may not be representative.

B.1 REPORTED NUMBER OF CITIZEN COMPLAINTS OF EXCESSIVE FORCE RECEIVED

Tables B-11.1 and B-11.2 present the number of citizen complaints of excessive force that responding agencies reported they received in 1991. Table B-11.1 provides these numbers for each agency type and Table B-11.2 provides these numbers for each agency type by size.

This information on the actual number of complaints reported by agencies in the survey is useful for understanding the sources and thus representativeness of these data, which are presented as rates in a following section. The figures are not weighted.

Table B-11.1 indicates that a total of 840 agencies (75.6 percent of all responding agencies) provided data concerning the number of citizen complaints of excessive force received in 1991. This included 215 sheriffs' departments (71.0%), 25 county police departments (78.1%), 568 city police departments (77.7%), and 32 state agencies (71.1%). The remaining agencies indicated that they did not maintain such information, that such information was kept but could not be made readily available, or that such information was confidential and could not be made public.

Among those agencies providing information, a total of 15,608 complaints of police use of excessive force were reported to have been received in 1991.

AGENCY TYPE

As shown in Table B-11.1, the largest number of complaints of excessive force was reported by responding city police departments; a total of 13,886 complaints were reported as having been received by 568 departments in 1991. This compared to 872 reported by 215 sheriffs' departments, 467 by 32 state agencies, and 383 by 25 county police departments.

AGENCY SIZE

Table B-11.2 provides the results for each agency type by agency size. Not surprisingly, in general, larger agencies, regardless of type, reported receiving the most complaints. The only exceptions to this were in the cases in which small numbers of agencies provided information, such as sheriffs' departments with 1,000 or more sworn officers.

B.2 DEMOGRAPHIC CHARACTERISTICS OF COMPLAINANTS AND OFFICERS

As indicated in the review of the literature presented earlier, there have been suggestions that the demographic characteristics of the persons filing complaints of excessive force may differ from those of the general population. In addition, the literature review has presented hypotheses that the demographic characteristics of officers against whom such complaints are filed may differ demographically from those of all officers.

In order to address these issues, law enforcement agencies were asked to provide information about the gender and race/ethnicity of persons filing complaints alleging excessive force in 1991 as well as of those whose complaints were sustained. For this analysis, this information was compared to data from the 1990 census.

In addition, agencies were asked to provide information about the gender, race/ethnicity, educational level, average age, and average time in service for all sworn officers, officers against whom citizen complaints of excessive force were filed in 1991, and officers against whom such complaints were sustained. For this analysis, the three distributions were compared.

The results of the comparisons of demographic characteristics of citizens and officers are presented below.

B.2.1 CITIZEN CHARACTERISTICS

Tables 8.1 through 8.4 provide information about the demographic characteristics of the general population served by agencies that provided citizen complaint data, as well as comparable information concerning the demographic characteristics of citizens who filed complaints of excessive force and of citizens whose complaints were sustained.

In interpreting these tables, it should be noted that, in accordance with Census Bureau coding, the persons categorized as Hispanic in the general population may be of any race. As a result, the percentage of the population listed as Hispanic should be considered separate from, not added to, the percentages in the other categories.

On the other hand, based on the results of the pre-test, law enforcement agencies were asked to categorize complainants according to mutually exclusive categories for race/ethnicity. Thus, the Hispanic category does not overlap with those for other race/ethnic groups.

B.2.1A SHERIFFS' DEPARTMENTS

As Table 8.1 indicates, the total population in the jurisdictions served by sheriffs' departments supplying demographic data about complainants consisted of 48.7 percent males and 51.3 percent females. Among complainants, however, 76.6 percent were males, indicating that males were much more likely to complain of excessive force than would have been the case if the gender distribution of complainants reflected that of the general population. Unfortunately, a more appropriate comparison figure, that for arrestees, was not available. Among citizens whose complaints of excessive force were sustained, 79.0 percent were males, indicating that complaints filed by males were marginally more likely to be sustained than were those filed by females.

Among the members of the general population served by the sheriffs' departments providing demographic data concerning complainants, 80.9 percent were white, 11.8 percent were black, 12.6 percent were Hispanic in origin, and the remaining 7.4 percent were of other

Table 8.1

Comparison of Demographic Characteristics Of General Population, Complainants, And Sustained Complainants: Sheriffs' Departments

Characteristic	Comparison Groups		
	General Population	Complainants	Sustained Complainants
Gender			
Male	14,164,346 (48.7)	423 (76.6)	49 (79.0)
Female	14,918,151 (51.3)	128 (23.2)	13 (21.0)
Total	29,082,497 (100.0)	551 (100.0)	62 (100.0)
Race/Ethnicity			
Black	3,417,768 (11.8)	121 (21.0)	15 (22.1)
Hispanic	[3,655,934*] (12.6)	51 (8.9)	8 (11.8)
Asian, American Indian, Other	2,151,219 (7.4)	11 (1.9)	2 (2.9)
White	23,513,510 (80.9)	392 (68.2)	43 (63.2)
Total	29,082,497 (100.0)	575 (100.0)	68 (100.0)
Total Responding Agencies	90	90	43

*In the general population data, Hispanics may be of any race

92

racial or ethnic origin. Among complainants, however, 68.2 percent were white, 21.0 percent were black, 8.9 percent were of Hispanic origin, and 1.9 percent were of other origins. Thus, compared to the general population, whites and those of "other" origins were somewhat under-represented among complainants, and blacks were considerably overrepresented. As with the figures describing the gender representation above, the figures denoting representation in the general population likely do not reflect race/ethnicity representation in police-citizen encounters.

Among those whose complaints of excessive force were sustained, 63.2 percent were white, 22.1 percent were black, 11.8 percent were Hispanic, and 2.9 percent were of other origins. These percentages were not dissimilar from those of complainants in general.

B.2.1B COUNTY POLICE DEPARTMENTS

As shown by Table 8.2, the total population in the jurisdictions served by county police departments providing demographic data about complainants was made up of 48.4 percent males and 51.6 percent females. The gender composition of complainants, however, consisted of 67.2 percent males and 32.8 percent females, again indicating that males were overrepresented relative to the general population among those complaining of excessive force. Among citizens whose complaints of excessive force were sustained, 80.0 percent were males, compared to 20.0 percent of females, demonstrating that complaints filed by males were more likely to be sustained than were those filed by females.

Among the members of the general population served by the county police departments providing demographic data concerning complainants, 65.3 percent were white, 30.8 percent were black, 3.0 percent were Hispanic in origin, and the remaining 3.9 percent were of other racial or ethnic origin. Among complainants, however, 40.8 percent were white, 52.0 percent were black, 6.4 percent were of Hispanic origin, and 0.8 percent were of other origins. Thus, compared to the general population, whites were notably underrepresented among complainants and blacks were notably overrepresented.

Among persons whose complaints of excessive force were sustained, 83.3 percent were white and 16.7 percent were black. No other ethnic/race categories were represented. Thus, compared to all complainants, whites were markedly overrepresented among those with sustained complaints and blacks were considerably underrepresented.

B.2.1C CITY POLICE DEPARTMENTS

Table 8.3 indicates that among the total population in the jurisdictions served by city police departments providing demographic data about complainants, 47.8 percent were males and 52.2 percent females. Among complainants, 72.8 percent were males and 27.2 percent females, revealing a notable overrepresentation of males among those complaining of excessive force, relative to their representation in the general population. Among citizens whose complaints of excessive force were sustained, 82.9 percent were males and 17.1

Table 8.2

Comparison of Demographic Characteristics Of General Population, Complainants, And Sustained Complainants: County Police Departments

Characteristic	Comparison Groups		
	General Population	Complainants	Sustained Complainants
Gender			
Male	1,571,949 (48.4)	84 (67.2)	8 (80.0)
Female	1,672,669 (51.6)	41 (32.8)	2 (20.0)
Total	3,244,618 (100.0)	125 (100.0)	10 (100.0)
Race/Ethnicity			
Black	998,149 (30.8)	65 (52.0)	2 (16.7)
Hispanic	[98,683*] (3.0)	8 (6.4)	0 (0.0)
Asian, American Indian, Other	126,536 (3.9)	1 (0.8)	0 (0.0)
White	2,119,933 (65.3)	51 (40.8)	10 (83.3)
Total	3,244,618 (100.0)	125 (100.0)	12 (100.0)
Total Responding Agencies	9	9	9

*In the general population data, Hispanics may be of any race

94

Table 8.3

Comparison of Demographic Characteristics Of General Population, Complainants, And Sustained Complainants: City Police Departments

Characteristic	Comparison Groups		
	General Population	Complainants	Sustained Complainants
Gender			
Male	12,910,899 (47.8)	2,224 (72.8)	398 (82.9)
Female	14,125,190 (52.2)	829 (27.2)	82 (17.1)
Total	27,036,089 (100.0)	3,053 (100.0)	480 (100.0)
Race/Ethnicity			
Black	5,787,552 (21.4)	1,322 (42.3)	136 (27.3)
Hispanic	[3,956,959*] (14.6)	382 (12.2)	66 (13.2)
Asian, American Indian, Other	3,356,116 (12.4)	128 (4.1)	16 (3.2)
White	17,892,421 (66.2)	1,290 (41.3)	281 (56.3)
Total	27,036,089 (100.0)	3,122 (100.0)	499 (100.0)
Total Responding Agencies	215	215	173

*In the general population data, Hispanics may be of any race

percent females, indicating a slightly higher likelihood that complaints filed by males would be sustained.

Whites made up 66.2 percent of the general population served by the city police departments providing demographic data concerning complainants; blacks constituted 21.4 percent, Hispanics 14.6 percent, and others 12.4 percent. Among complainants, however, 41.3 percent were white, 42.3 percent were black, 12.2 percent were of Hispanic origin, and 4.1 percent were of other origins. These figures indicate that, compared to the general population, whites and those of "other" origins were underrepresented among complainants and blacks were overrepresented.

Among persons whose complaints of excessive force were sustained, 56.3 percent were white, 27.3 percent were black, 13.2 percent were Hispanic, and 3.2 percent were of other origins. Thus, compared to all complainants, whites were notably overrepresented among those with sustained complaints and blacks were somewhat underrepresented.

B.2.1D STATE AGENCIES

As shown in Table 8.4, males made up 48.5 percent of the total population in the jurisdictions served by the state law enforcement agencies providing demographic data about complainants; females constituted 51.5 percent. Among complainants, however, males were overrepresented relative to their representation in the general population, constituting 74.5 percent, compared to 25.5 percent who were females. Among citizens whose complaints of excessive force were sustained, 80.0 percent were males and 20.0 percent were females, indicating a slightly lower likelihood that complaints filed by males would be sustained.

Among the general population served by the state agencies providing demographic data concerning complainants, whites constituted 62.9 percent, blacks 14.1 percent, Hispanics 5.1 percent, and others 2.8 percent. Among complainants, whites made up 79.0 percent, blacks 12.9 percent, Hispanics 1.6 percent, and others 6.5 percent. Thus, the racial/ethnic composition of complainants was generally similar to that of the general population, except that whites and persons of "other" origin were slightly overrepresented among complainants, and blacks and Hispanics were slightly underrepresented.

Among those whose complaints were sustained, whites made up 70.0 percent, blacks 25.0 percent, and Hispanics 5.0 percent. White complainants, then, were somewhat less likely to have their complaints sustained than either blacks or Hispanics.

B.2.2 OFFICER CHARACTERISTICS

Tables 9.1 through 9.4 provide information about the demographic characteristics of all sworn officers in the agencies that provided citizen complaint data, as well as comparable information concerning the demographic characteristics of officers against whom citizen complaints of excessive force were filed and of officers against whom such complaints were sustained. Unfortunately, demographics for all sworn *field* officers were not consistently

Table 8.4

Comparison of Demographic Characteristics Of General Population, Complainants, And Sustained Complainants: State Agencies

Characteristic	Comparison Groups		
	General Population	Complainants	Sustained Complainants
Gender			
Male	23,879,816 (48.5)	41 (74.5)	16 (80.0)
Female	25,328,126 (51.5)	14 (25.5)	4 (20.0)
Total	49,207,942 (100.0)	55 (100.0)	20 (100.0)
Race/Ethnicity			
Black	6,917,576 (14.1)	8 (12.9)	5 (25.0)
Hispanic	[2,524,428*] (5.1)	1 (1.6)	1 (5.0)
Asian, American Indian, Other	1,354,553 (2.8)	4 (6.5)	0 (0.0)
White	30,935,813 (62.9)	49 (79.0)	14 (70.0)
Total	49,207,942 (100.0)	62 (100.0)	20 (100.0)
Total Responding Agencies	14	14	9

*In the general population data, Hispanics may be of any race

provided by responding agencies. Field officers would have been the more appropriate baseline comparison group for these analyses.

Unlike the preceding analyses of citizen characteristics, the race/ethnic characteristics of officers were provided according to mutually exclusive categories. As a result, Hispanic officers were not also included in any other category.

B.2.2A SHERIFFS' DEPARTMENTS

Table 9.1 provides demographic data concerning officers in those sheriffs' departments that supplied the requisite information about citizen complaints of excessive force. As that table shows, among all sworn officers in those departments, 85.9 percent were male, compared to 92.6 percent of officers against whom citizen complaints of excessive force were filed, and 96.3 percent of officers against whom such complaints were sustained. These results indicate that male officers were somewhat more likely than female officers to receive complaints. In addition, these data suggest, complaints against male officers were slightly more likely to be sustained than were those against female officers.

Among all officers in the sheriffs' departments supplying the necessary data, whites constituted 80.1 percent, blacks 7.7 percent, Hispanics 10.6 percent, and persons of other race/ethnic category made up less than two percent. Among officers against whom complaints of excessive force were filed, whites made up 80.9 percent, blacks 6.2 percent, and Hispanics 11.6 percent. Thus, the officers against whom citizens complained were representative of all officers in those departments in terms of race/ethnicity. Similarly, no race/ethnicity was disproportionately represented among officers against whom complaints were sustained.

Among all sworn officers in the sheriffs' departments involved in this analysis, 17.4 percent had graduated with at least a B.A. or a B.S. degree, compared to 8.5 percent of those against whom complaints were filed. These results indicate that college-educated officers were underrepresented among officers receiving complaints. However, among officers against whom complaints were sustained, 17.1 percent had at least a B.A. or B.S. degree—the same as among all sworn officers.

The average age of all sworn officers in the sheriffs' departments providing data concerning citizen complaints was 36.2. Among officers against whom complaints of excessive force were filed, the average age was 31.8. Officers against whom such complaints were sustained had an average age of 32.0. These results indicate that, on average, officers receiving citizen complaints, and having those complaints sustained, were slightly younger than sworn officers in general.

Similar results were found with respect to the time in service, with the average among all sworn officers being 8.9 years, compared to 6.2 years among officers against whom complaints were lodged, and 6.6 years among officers against whom complaints were sustained.

Table 9.1

Comparison of Demographic Characteristics
Of All Sworn Officers, with Citizen Complaints, and Officers with Sustained Complaints:
Sheriffs' Departments

Characteristic	Comparison Groups		
	All Sworn Officers	Officers with Citizen Complaints	Officers with Sustained Complaints
Gender			
Male	26,692 (85.9)	870 (92.6)	79 (96.3)
Female	4,383 (14.1)	70 (7.4)	3 (3.7)
Total	31,075 (100.0)	940 (100.0)	82 (100.0)
Ethnicity/Race			
Black	2,400 (7.7)	63 (6.2)	6 (7.0)
Hispanic	3,299 (10.6)	117 (11.6)	11 (12.8)
Other	472 (1.5)	13 (1.3)	1 (1.2)
White	24,903 (80.1)	817 (80.9)	68 (79.1)
Total	31,074 (100.0)	1,010 (100.0)	86 (100.0)
Education			
Advanced Degree	150 (2.4)	2 (1.0)	0 (0.0)
BA/BS Degree	1,104 (17.4)	17 (8.5)	7 (17.1)
Associate Degree	1,005 (15.9)	29 (14.4)	9 (22.0)
Less than 2 Years College	1,268 (20.0)	37 (18.4)	4 (9.8)
High School	2,806 (44.3)	116 (57.7)	21 (51.2)
Total	6,333 (100.0)	201 (100.0)	41 (100.0)
Average Age	36.20	31.78	32.00
Average Time in Service	8.89	6.16	6.55

B.2.2B County Police Departments

As shown in Table 9.2, 89.0 percent of the sworn officers in those county police departments that supplied the necessary information were males, compared to 96.4 percent of those officers against whom complaints of excessive force were filed, and 100 percent of those against whom such complaints were sustained. Thus, male officers were overrepresented among both those receiving complaints and those against whom complaints were sustained.

Among all officers in the county police departments supplying the necessary data, whites constituted 80.3 percent, blacks 17.5 percent, Hispanics 1.6 percent, and persons of other types made up less than one percent. Among officers against whom complaints of excessive force were filed, whites made up 73.9 percent, blacks 23.6 percent, and Hispanics 1.8 percent. Thus, white officers were somewhat underrepresented among officers receiving complaints, while blacks were slightly overrepresented. Hispanic officers represented approximately the same percentage of total sworn officers and of officers receiving complaints.

White officers made up 92.0 percent of officers against whom complaints of excessive force were sustained, while black officers made up 4.0 percent, and officers of other, non-Hispanic, backgrounds made up the remaining 4.0 percent. These results indicate that, although white officers were underrepresented among officers receiving complaints, they were somewhat overrepresented among officers against whom complaints were sustained. Black officers present the opposite pattern of being overrepresented among officers receiving complaints but underrepresented among those against whom complaints were sustained.

Among all sworn county police officers, 13.8 percent had more than a high school degree but less than 2 years of college, compared to 22.6 percent of those against whom complaints were filed, and 29.4 percent of those against whom such complaints were sustained. The percentage of officers with high school degrees was 33.5 among the sworn officers, 15.1 among officers against whom complaints were filed, and 41.2 among officers against whom complaints were sustained. Thus, officers with less than two years of college were overrepresented among both officers with citizen complaints and officers against whom complaints were sustained. Officers with high school degrees were underrepresented among officers with citizen complaints but overrepresented among officers against whom complaints were sustained.

The average age of all sworn officers in the county police departments providing the necessary data was 34.4. Among officers against whom complaints of excessive force were filed, the average age was 31.3. The average age of officers against whom such complaints were sustained was 33.5. Thus, officers against whom complaints were sustained were representative of all sworn officers in the departments in terms of age. Average time in service was 8.7 for all officers in the departments providing data, 5.9 among the officers with citizen complaints, and 7.8 among officers against whom complaints were sustained. Thus less experienced officers were somewhat overrepresented among the group of officers against whom citizen complaints were filed and slightly overrepresented among the group of officers against whom complaints were sustained.

Table 9.2

Comparison of Demographic Characteristics
Of All Sworn Officers, with Citizen Complaints, and Officers with Sustained Complaints: County Police Departments

Characteristic	Comparison Groups		
	All Sworn Officers	Officers with Citizen Complaints	Officers with Sustained Complaints
Gender			
Male	4,772 (89.0)	264 (96.4)	23 (100.0)
Female	590 (11.0)	10 (3.6)	0 (0.0)
Total	5,362 (100.0)	274 (100.0)	23 (100.0)
Ethnicity/Race			
Black	937 (17.5)	65 (23.6)	1 (4.0)
Hispanic	84 (1.6)	5 (1.8)	0 (0.0)
Other	34 (0.6)	2 (0.7)	1 (4.0)
White	4,307 (80.3)	204 (73.9)	23 (92.0)
Total	5,362 (100.0)	276 (100.0)	25 (100.0)
Education			
Advanced Degree	40 (3.2)	0 (0.0)	0 (0.0)
BA/BS Degree	446 (35.4)	19 (35.8)	4 (23.5)
Associate Degree	178 (14.1)	14 (26.4)	1 (5.9)
Less than 2 Years College	174 (13.8)	12 (22.6)	5 (29.4)
High School	422 (33.5)	8 (15.1)	7 (41.2)
Total	1,260 (100.0)	53 (100.0)	17 (100.0)
Average Age	34.43	31.29	33.54
Average Time in Service	8.71	5.86	7.75

B.2.2C City Police Departments

Table 9.3 provides data concerning the demographic characteristics of officers in those city police departments that provided data concerning demographic characteristics of officers against whom citizens filed complaints of excessive force. As that table indicates, 88.6 percent of the sworn officers in those departments were males, compared to 95.8 percent of those officers against whom complaints were filed, and 95.4 percent of those against whom such complaints were sustained. Thus, male officers were overrepresented among both those receiving complaints and those against whom complaints were sustained.

Among all sworn city police officers, whites constituted 77.8 percent, blacks 13.3 percent, Hispanics 8.0 percent, and persons of other categories 1.0 percent. Among officers against whom complaints of excessive force were filed, whites made up 68.4 percent, blacks 12.5 percent, Hispanics 10.4 percent, and others 8.7 percent. White officers were slightly underrepresented among those receiving complaints and persons of "other" race/ethnicity were slightly overrepresented.

White officers made up 73.2 percent of officers against whom complaints of excessive force were sustained, black officers made up 17.3 percent, Hispanic officers constituted 8.4 percent, and officers of other, non-Hispanic, backgrounds made up 1.1 percent. Thus, the racial/ethnic distribution of officers against whom complaints were sustained was approximately the same as that of all sworn officers.

Among all sworn municipal officers, persons with associate degrees or with less than two years of college were somewhat overrepresented among both officers against whom complaints were filed and among officers against whom complaints were sustained. In contrast, those with B.A./B.S. degrees or with only high school degrees were somewhat underrepresented.

The average age of all sworn officers in the departments providing the necessary data was 35.9. Among officers against whom complaints of excessive force were filed, the average age was 31.2. Among officers against whom complaints were sustained, the average age was 31.6. As found with previous analyses, therefore, city police officers receiving citizen complaints, and having those complaints sustained, were younger, on average, than officers in general.

Among all sworn officers, the average time in service was 10.3 years, compared to 6.6 years among those against whom complaints were lodged, and 6.6 years among those against whom complaints were sustained. Thus, as with earlier analyses, officers receiving complaints as well as those against whom complaints were sustained, tended to have served fewer years in the department than the average officer.

Table 9.3

Comparison of Demographic Characteristics
Of All Sworn Officers, with Citizen Complaints, and Officers with Sustained Complaints:
City Police Departments

Characteristic	Comparison Groups		
	All Sworn Officers	Officers with Citizen Complaints	Officers with Sustained Complaints
Gender			
Male	88,231 (88.6)	8,042 (95.8)	397 (95.4)
Female	13,313 (11.4)	352 (4.2)	19 (4.6)
Total	99,544 (100.0)	8,394 (100.0)	416 (100.0)
Ethnicity/Race			
Black	12,742 (13.3)	1,037 (12.5)	76 (17.3)
Hispanic	7,672 (8.0)	857 (10.4)	37 (8.4)
Other	927 (1.0)	720 (8.7)	5 (1.1)
White	74,626 (77.8)	5,658 (68.4)	322 (73.2)
Total	95,961 (100.0)	8,272 (100.0)	440 (100.0)
Education			
Advanced Degree	663 (2.6)	21 (1.3)	6 (2.1)
BA/BS Degree	4,998 (19.7)	285 (18.3)	37 (12.9)
Associate Degree	3,491 (13.8)	279 (17.9)	54 (18.8)
Less than 2 Years College	5,616 (22.2)	411 (26.4)	79 (27.5)
High School	10,539 (41.6)	563 (36.1)	111 (38.7)
Total	25,307 (100.0)	1,559 (100.0)	287 (100.0)
Average Age	35.85	31.24	31.55
Average Time in Service	10.30	6.55	6.59

B.2.2D STATE AGENCIES

As indicated in Table 9.4, males constituted 95.1 percent of all sworn officers in state law enforcement agencies that provided demographic data concerning officers receiving citizen complaints. This compares to 95.7 percent of those officers against whom citizen complaints of excessive force were filed and 94.9 percent of those officers against whom such complaints were sustained. Thus, in state law enforcement agencies, males were not overrepresented among those receiving complaints or those against whom complaints were sustained.

Among all sworn officers in state law enforcement agencies analyzed, whites made up 85.4 percent, blacks 8.7 percent, Hispanics 5.1 percent, and persons of other race/ethnic categories less than one percent. Among officers against whom complaints of excessive force were filed, whites made up 79.8 percent, blacks 13.6 percent, Hispanics 6.3 percent, and others less than one percent. Thus, white officers were slightly underrepresented among those receiving complaints, while black officers were somewhat overrepresented.

White officers made up 72.5 percent of those against whom complaints of excessive force were sustained, black officers made up 15.0 percent, and Hispanic officers constituted 12.5 percent. The results indicate that among officers against whom complaints were sustained, the white officers were somewhat underrepresented, and black and Hispanic officers were somewhat overrepresented.

Among all sworn state officers, 31.5 percent had received at least a B.A. or a B.S. degree, compared to 31.4 percent of those against whom complaints were filed, and 22.7 percent of those against whom such complaints were sustained. Thus, college-educated officers were underrepresented among officers against whom complaints were sustained. Although officers with associate's degrees were overrepresented among officers with citizen complaints, they were proportionately represented among officers against whom complaints were sustained. Officers with less than two years of college accounted for 40.7 percent of all officers in the departments providing data, 27.5 percent of the officers against whom complaints were filed, and 27.3 percent of the officers against whom complaints were sustained. Thus, officers with two years of college were underrepresented among persons with complaints and persons with sustained complaints. Officers with high school degrees were underrepresented among officers with citizen complaints but greatly overrepresented among officers against whom complaints were sustained. Whereas officers with high school degrees accounted for 10.2 percent of all officers, they accounted for 36.4 percent of all officers against whom complaints were sustained.

The average age of all sworn state law enforcement officers in agencies providing citizen complaint data was 31.3, compared to 32.7 among officers against whom complaints were filed, and 35.0 among officers against whom complaints were sustained. Thus, unlike the findings with other agency types, the average ages of state officers against whom complaints of excessive force were filed, and of those against whom complaints were sustained, were somewhat higher than that of officers in general, although the differences were small.

Table 9.4

Comparison of Demographic Characteristics
Of All Sworn Officers, with Citizen Complaints, and Officers with Sustained Complaints:
State Agencies

Characteristic	Comparison Groups		
	All Sworn Officers	Officers with Citizen Complaints	Officers with Sustained Complaints
Gender			
Male	24,826 (95.1)	576 (95.7)	37 (94.9)
Female	1,267 (4.9)	26 (4.3)	2 (5.1)
Total	26,093 (100.0)	602 (100.0)	39 (100.0)
Ethnicity/Race			
Black	2,312 (8.7)	82 (13.6)	6 (15.0)
Hispanic	1,332 (5.1)	38 (6.3)	5 (12.5)
Other	159 (0.6)	2 (0.3)	0 (0.0)
White	22,256 (85.4)	483 (79.8)	29 (72.5)
Total	26,059 (100.0)	605 (100.0)	40 (100.0)
Education			
Advanced Degree	5 (2.6)	0 (0.0)	0 (0.0)
BA/BS Degree	656 (31.5)	16 (31.4)	5 (22.7)
Associate Degree	313 (15.0)	19 (37.3)	3 (13.6)
Less than 2 Years College	848 (40.7)	14 (27.5)	6 (27.3)
High School	212 (10.2)	2 (3.9)	8 (36.4)
Total	2,084 (100.0)	51 (100.0)	22 (100.0)
Average Age	31.33	32.67	35.00
Average Time in Service	19.67	9.67	9.25

Among all sworn state officers in the agencies providing citizen complaint data, the average time in service was 19.7 years, compared to 9.7 years among those against whom complaints were filed, and 9.3 years among those against whom complaints of excessive force were sustained. These findings are consistent with those among the other agency types, with officers receiving complaints as well as those against whom complaints were sustained having served fewer years in the department than the average officer.

B.3 REPORTED COMPLAINTS RECEIVED PER 1,000 SWORN OFFICERS

In order to standardize the absolute number of complaints, a new indicator was created representing the number of complaints of excessive force received for every 1,000 sworn personnel. As with the measures concerning use of force, this measure was calculated by dividing the total number of complaints received by the number of sworn officers and multiplying the result by 1,000. Weighted results from analyses of such standardized measures are provided in Tables 10.1 and 10.2 and in Figures 11, 12.1 and 12.2. These data were supplied by 215 sheriffs' departments (71.0% of the sheriffs' departments that responded to the survey), 25 county police departments (78.1%), 568 city police departments (77.7%), and 32 state agencies (71.1%).

AGENCY TYPE

As indicated in Figure 11, city police departments reported the highest number of complaints received per 1,000 sworn officers (47.5), followed by 33.8 among county police departments, 20.7 among sheriffs' departments, and 15.7 among state agencies.

AGENCY SIZE

Results by agency type and size are contained in Table 10.2 and Figures 12.1 and 12.2 for both sheriffs' departments and municipal agencies. The three top agency size categories were combined for the sheriffs' departments due to the small number of agencies within those cells. (Table B-12 contains the complete agency size breakdowns for sheriffs' departments, as well as the agency size information for county police departments and state agencies.) There was no clear relationship between agency size and the per officer rate at which excessive force complaints were received among sheriffs' departments.

Among city police departments, larger agencies generally reported higher rates of complaints than did smaller ones. The highest rates, for example, were reported by agencies in the two largest size categories. The lowest rate (25.0 per 1,000) was reported by departments with between 25 and 49 sworn officers. Agencies in the smallest size category, with fewer than 25 sworn officers, were an exception to the general trend, with a reported complaint rate (49.7 per 1,000) as high as the mid-sized agencies.

Table 10.1

Citizen Complaints of Excessive Force Received in 1991 per 1,000 Sworn Officers: By Agency Type

Excessive Force Complaints	Agency Type			
	Sheriffs' Departments	County Police Departments	City Police Departments	State Agencies
Complaints per 1,000 Sworn Officers	20.7	33.8	47.5	15.7

NOTE: Rates are weighted

Table 10.2

Citizen Complaints of Excessive Force Received in 1991 per 1,000 Sworn Officers: By Agency Type and Size

Complaints per 1,000 Sworn Officers	Number of Sworn Personnel					
	1-24	25-49	50-99	100-249	250 or more	WRR*
Sheriffs' Departments	22.8 (46)	15.5 (31)	12.2 (47)	25.7 (53)	20.4 (38)	20.7

Complaints per 1,000 Sworn Officers	Number of Sworn Personnel						
	1-24	25-49	50-99	100-249	250-499	500-999	1,000 or more	WRR*
City Police Departments	49.7 (117)	25.0 (77)	45.5 (121)	68.8 (154)	74.8 (50)	90.8 (23)	91.2 (26)	47.5

* Weighted Row Rate

NOTE: Numbers in parentheses represent numbers of agencies providing responses

Figure 11: Reported 1991 Citizen Complaints of Excessive Force per 1,000 Sworn Officers: By Agency Type

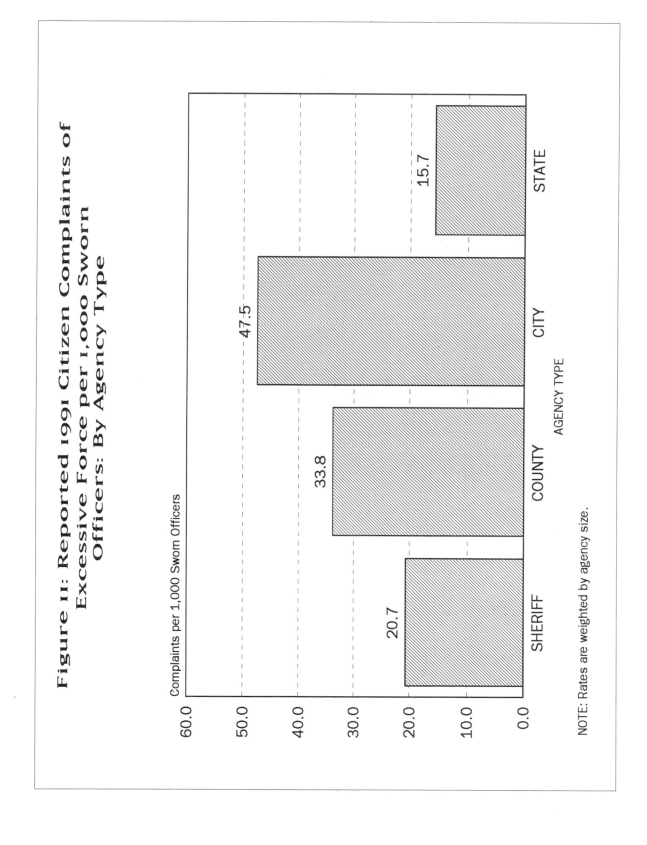

Complaints per 1,000 Sworn Officers

SHERIFF	20.7
COUNTY	33.8
CITY	47.5
STATE	15.7

AGENCY TYPE

NOTE: Rates are weighted by agency size.

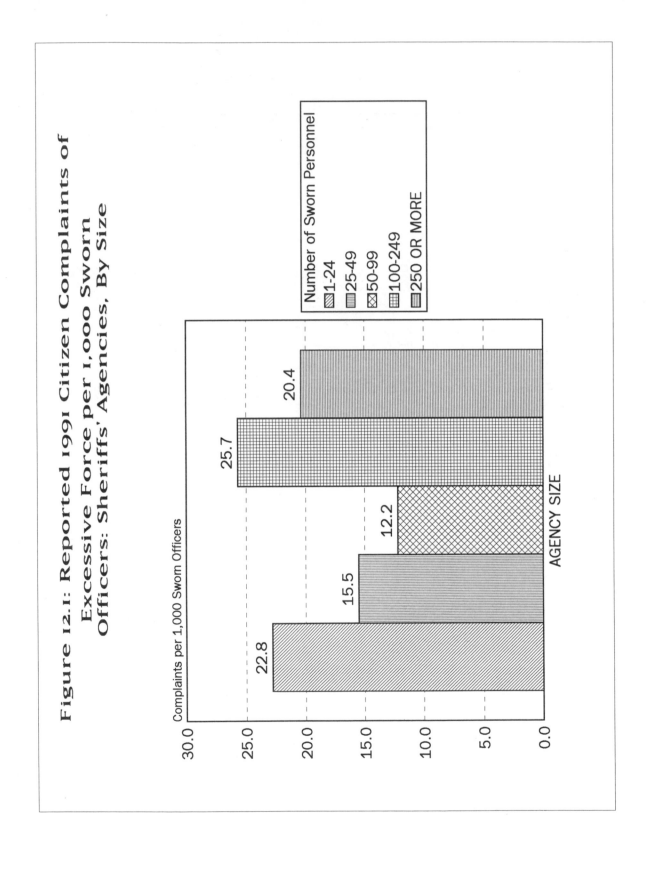

Figure 12.1: Reported 1991 Citizen Complaints of Excessive Force per 1,000 Sworn Officers: Sheriffs' Agencies, By Size

Complaints per 1,000 Sworn Officers

30.0
25.0
20.0
15.0
10.0
5.0
0.0

22.8

15.5

12.2

25.7

20.4

AGENCY SIZE

Number of Sworn Personnel
1-24
25-49
50-99
100-249
250 OR MORE

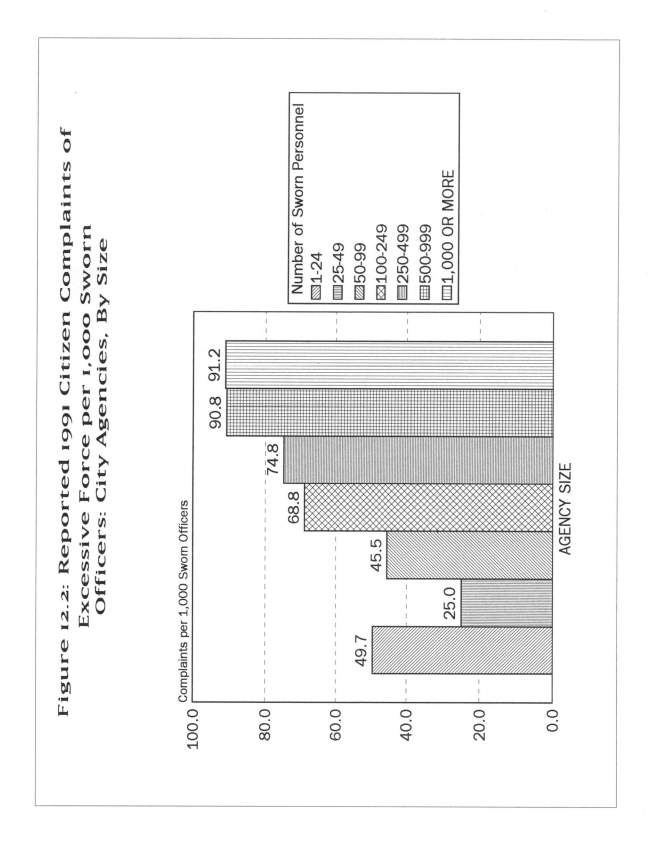

Figure 12.2: Reported 1991 Citizen Complaints of Excessive Force per 1,000 Sworn Officers: City Agencies, By Size

B.4 DISPOSITION OF COMPLAINTS

Agencies were requested to indicate the disposition of each citizen complaint of excessive force received in 1991. In particular, agencies were asked to provide information about whether the complaint was "unfounded" (i.e., that the complaint was found not to be based on fact or that the reported incident did not occur), the officer against whom the complaint was made was "exonerated" (i.e., that the incident occurred but the action taken by the officer was lawful and proper), the complaint was "not sustained" (i.e., there was insufficient evidence to prove or disprove the allegation), or the complaint was "sustained" (i.e., the allegation was supported by sufficient evidence to justify disciplinary action). In addition, agencies were allowed to indicate that the status of the complaint was still "pending," awaiting final disposition, or that there had been an "other" disposition. Based on information provided in the questionnaires and in subsequent telephone interviews, it has been determined that the "other" responses primarily referred to complaints that were withdrawn by the citizens prior to final disposition.

The Police Foundation adopted the above named categories because they appeared to best reflect the disposition terminology used by most agencies. Clear definitions of these terms were included in the questionnaire itself. It should be noted, however, that those categorizations are not universally used and/or consistently defined by departments and thus, the reliability and validity of these data may be affected by the different ways departments categorized their dispositions in responding to the survey.

As indicated above, 840 agencies provided information about citizen complaints of excessive force. Among those reporting such information, 830 also provided complete information about the disposition of those complaints. This included 215 sheriffs' departments, 25 county police departments, 558 city police departments, and 32 state agencies.

In the discussion that follows, the disposition of citizen complaints of excessive force will be analyzed in two ways. First, all dispositions will be examined, including those cases that are pending as well as those that received "other" dispositions. Thus, "pending" and "other" dispositions are included in the discussion of "Preliminary Dispositions" in section B.4.1.

The second analysis will consider only those cases that have been subjected to complete scrutiny of the complaint review process; these will be termed "Final Dispositions." Results of these analyses, which exclude "pending" and "other" dispositions, are presented in section B.4.2.

B.4.1   PRELIMINARY DISPOSITIONS

Tables 11.1 through 11.3 and B-13.1 through B-13.3 present the "preliminary disposition" results by agency type and by agency type and size.

AGENCY TYPE

The highest (weighted) percentages of sustained complaints were among state agencies and city police departments. State agencies reported that 12.2 percent of the excessive force complaints filed in 1991 were sustained; the corresponding figure for city police departments was 10.1.

Between 29.4 and 50.6 percent of the complaints within each agency type were determined to be "unfounded," and in another one-quarter to one-third, the officer was exonerated. The sheriffs' departments had the highest percentage of complaints determined to be "unfounded" (50.6 %) and city police departments had the highest percentage in which the officer was exonerated (35.3%).

Nine percent (8.9%) of the complaints reported by the county police departments were still pending by the time the survey was completed. This was higher than the corresponding figures for city police departments, sheriffs' departments, and state agencies, which reported pending percentages of 3.2, 1.8, and 0.4, respectively.

AGENCY SIZE

As shown in Table 11.2 (see also B-13.1), there was little variation across sheriffs' departments based on size in terms of the disposition of sustained complaints. Two exceptions were that larger departments (with 250 or more sworn personnel) had proportionately greater percentages of complaints that were "not sustained" and the smaller agencies had proportionately greater percentages of complaints determined to be "unfounded."

Among city police departments, as seen in Table 11.3, those with 250 or more sworn personnel had greater proportions of complaints that were "not sustained." The smaller departments, instead, indicated greater percentages of complaints in which the officer was exonerated. The largest agencies (with 1,000 or more sworn personnel) reported that 29.3 percent of their 1991 excessive force dispositions were "other" than those listed on the survey. Among the departments with fewer than 1,000 sworn officers, the number of complaints receiving "other" dispositions was between zero and 9.1 percent.

Tables B-13.2 and B-13.3 contain agency size information for county police departments and state agencies, respectively.

Table 11.1

**Preliminary Dispositions of Excessive Force Complaints:
By Agency Type**

Disposition	Agency Type			
	Sheriffs' Departments	County Police Departments	City Police Departments	State Agencies
Unfounded	50.6%	29.4%	33.7%	43.5%
Officer Exonerated	25.9	24.0	35.3	21.6
Not Sustained	14.3	28.6	17.4	21.2
Sustained	6.2	8.1	10.1	12.2
Pending	1.8	8.9	3.2	0.4
Other	1.3	1.0	0.3	1.1
Total	100.0	100.0	100.0	100.0

NOTE: Percentages are weighted

Table 11.2

Preliminary Dispositions of Excessive Force Complaints: Sheriffs' Departments by Agency Size

Disposition	Number of Sworn Personnel					WCP*
	1-24	25-49	50-99	100-249	250 or more	
Unfounded	7 (53.8)	6 (40.0)	25 (61.0)	87 (39.9)	175 (30.1)	50.6
Officer Exonerated	3 (23.1)	6 (40.0)	7 (17.1)	62 (28.4)	164 (28.2)	25.9
Not Sustained	2 (15.4)	1 (6.7)	5 (12.2)	40 (18.3)	183 (31.4)	14.3
Sustained	1 (7.7)	0 (0.0)	2 (4.9)	21 (9.6)	30 (5.2)	6.2
Pending	0 (0.0)	1 (6.7)	2 (4.9)	7 (3.2)	8 (1.4)	1.8
Other	0 (0.0)	1 (6.7)	0 (0.0)	1 (0.5)	22 (3.8)	1.3
Total	13 (100.0)	15 (100.0)	41 (100.0)	218 (100.0)	582 (100.0)	100.0
Total Responding Agencies	46	31	47	53	38	

* Weighted Column Percent

NOTE: Column totals may not sum to 100.0% due to rounding

Table 11.3

**Preliminary Dispositions of Excessive Force Complaints:
City Police Departments by Agency Size**

Disposition	Number of Sworn Personnel							
	1-24	25-49	50-99	100-249	250-499	500-999	1,000 or more	WCP*
Unfounded	19 (32.2)	32 (45.1)	148 (35.7)	479 (30.3)	285 (22.9)	222 (18.3)	557 (11.2)	33.7
Officer Exonerated	22 (37.3)	20 (28.2)	131 (31.6)	349 (22.1)	400 (32.2)	267 (22.0)	392 (7.9)	35.3
Not Sustained	10 (16.9)	10 (14.1)	80 (19.3)	533 (33.7)	373 (30.0)	481 (39.6)	2,137 (43.0)	17.4
Sustained	6 (10.2)	7 (9.9)	43 (10.4)	133 (8.4)	79 (6.4)	66 (5.4)	226 (4.6)	10.1
Pending	2 (3.4)	2 (2.8)	5 (1.2)	27 (1.7)	58 (4.7)	68 (5.6)	197 (4.0)	3.2
Other	0 (0.0)	0 (0.0)	8 (1.9)	61 (3.9)	49 (3.9)	111 (9.1)	1,455 (29.3)	0.3
Total	59 (100.0)	71 (100.0)	415 (100.0)	1,582 (100.0)	1,244 (100.0)	1,215 (100.0)	4,964 (100.0)	100.0
Total Responding Agencies	117	77	120	152	50	21	21	

* Weighted Column Percent

NOTE: Column totals may not sum to 100.0% due to rounding

B.4.2   FINAL DISPOSITIONS

Between 0.4 and 8.9 percent of the excessive force complaints for which dispositions were provided for each agency type were still pending at the time the survey was submitted. An additional 0.3 to 1.3 percent had an "other" disposition (again, this category referred primarily to complaints withdrawn). As such, table percentages of sustained complaints were dependent in part on the number of complaints still pending and those that fell into the "other" category. To remove the effects of these categories, Figures 13, 14.1 and 14.2 provide graphic presentations of the percent of complaints of excessive force that were sustained, based on the number of sustained complaints from among all the complaints receiving one of the four major dispositions—unfounded, exonerated, not sustained, and sustained. That is, the calculations for these figures did not include in the denominator the complaints that were pending or the complaints that were withdrawn. These new percentages are thus, by definition, larger than the percent sustained figures described above and allow for an alternative way to compare dispositions across agency type and size.

AGENCY TYPE

Figure 13 indicates, for each agency type, the weighted percentage of the excessive force complaints (resulting in a valid disposition) that were sustained. As that figure shows, state agencies reported the highest percent of complaints that had been sustained (12.4%). This compared to sustained percentages of 10.4, 8.5, and 6.1 for city police departments, county police departments, and sheriffs' departments, respectively.

AGENCY SIZE

Figure 14.1 provides information concerning the percentage of complaints that were sustained, as a final disposition, by sheriffs' departments by agency size. (Sheriffs' agencies within the top three size categories were grouped together to provide adequate cell frequencies.) The percentages sustained ranged from 0.0 among agencies with 25 to 49 sworn personnel to 10.0 among agencies with 100 to 249 sworn personnel. There was no apparent relationship between agency size and the percent of complaints that were sustained.

In contrast, there appeared to be an inverse relationship between agency size and the percent of complaints that were sustained among the city police departments. As indicated in Figure 14.2, the smallest city agencies—those with 1 to 24, 25 to 49, and 50 to 99 sworn personnel—sustained 10.5, 10.1, and 10.7 percent of the complaints they received in 1991, respectively. Among the largest agencies—those with 250 to 499, 500 to 999, and 1,000 or more sworn personnel—the corresponding percentages ranged from 6.4 to 6.9.

Figure 13: Final Disposition of 1991 Citizen Complaints of Excessive Force: Percent Sustained By Agency Type

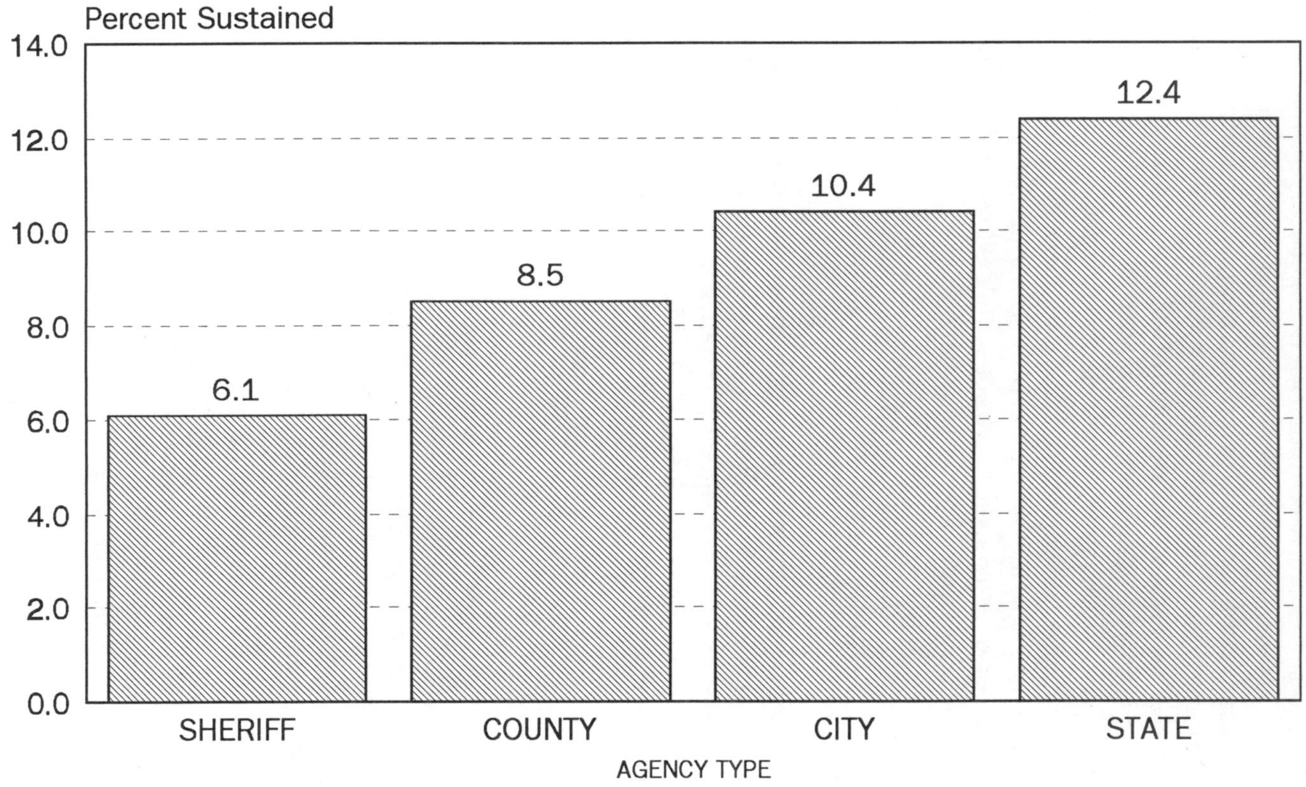

Percent Sustained

	6.1	8.5	10.4	12.4
	SHERIFF	COUNTY	CITY	STATE

AGENCY TYPE

NOTE: Rates are weighted by agency size.

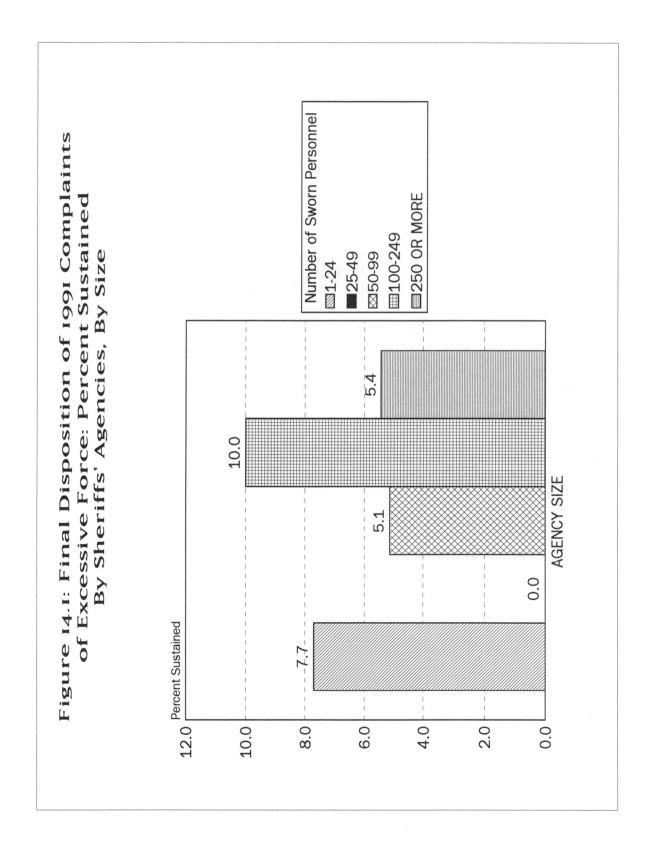

Figure 14.1: Final Disposition of 1991 Complaints of Excessive Force: Percent Sustained By Sheriffs' Agencies, By Size

Number of Sworn Personnel
- 1-24
- 25-49
- 50-99
- 100-249
- 250 OR MORE

Percent Sustained

AGENCY SIZE

7.7 0.0 5.1 10.0 5.4

12.0 10.0 8.0 6.0 4.0 2.0 0.0

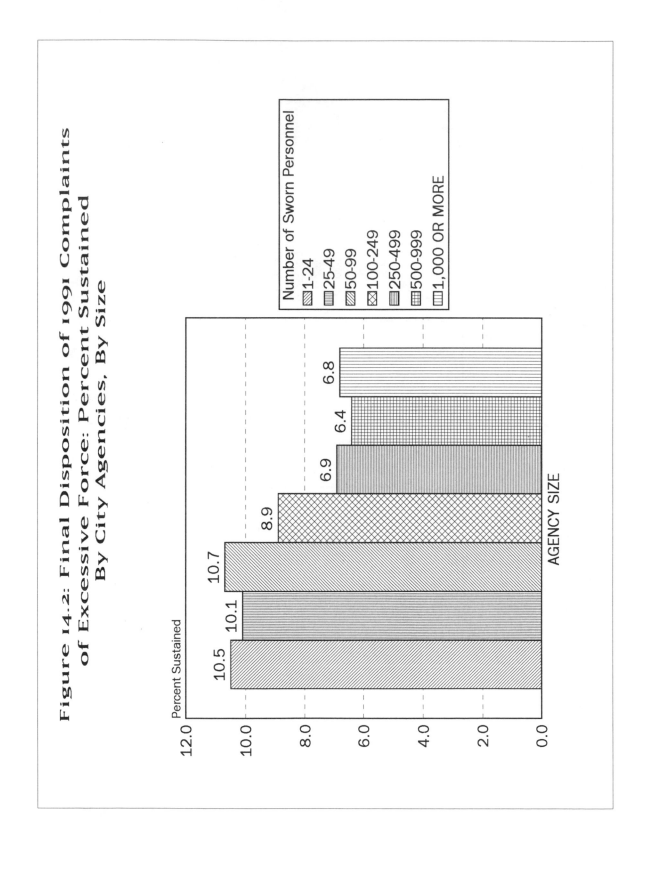

Figure 14.2: Final Disposition of 1991 Complaints of Excessive Force: Percent Sustained By City Agencies, By Size

B.5 Discipline Administered Following Sustained Complaints of Excessive Force

Thirty-nine sheriffs' departments, 194 city police departments, 14 county police departments, and 20 state agencies provided data regarding the discipline that was administered following complaints that were sustained in 1991. These results are provided in Tables 12.1 through 12.3 and B-14.1 through B-14.4.

Agency Type

The plurality of sustained complaints of sheriffs' departments and state agencies resulted in reprimands. For county police departments and city police departments, the plurality of complaints resulted in suspensions.

Resulting in reprimands were 75.7 percent of the complaints from state agencies, 41.9 percent of the complaints from sheriffs' departments, 32.6 percent of the complaints from city police departments, and 17.3 percent of the complaints from county police departments.

Resulting in suspensions were 50.0 percent, 41.8 percent, 17.8 percent, and 13.6 percent of the complaints from the county police departments, city police departments, sheriffs' departments, and state agencies, respectively.

Between 0 and 5.3 percent of the complaints resulted in reassignment and between 6.2 and 17.6 percent resulted in termination.

Between 2 and 21 percent of the agencies within each type indicated that the disposition was "other" than the four traditional dispositions. Agencies indicated that these alternative resolutions included officers resigning or retiring, officers losing compensatory time, or referral of the case to the criminal justice system.

Agency Size

Tables 12.2 (see also B-14.1) and 12.3 (see also B-14.3) provide information regarding disciplinary action for sustained complaints for sheriffs' departments and city police departments by agency size. With disciplinary information from just 39 departments, it was necessary to combine size categories among sheriffs' departments before drawing any conclusions. After doing so, it appears that the agencies with 100 or more sworn personnel were more likely to impose a sanction of suspension than those agencies with fewer than 100 sworn personnel.

Size categories (1-24 and 25-49) were also combined for the city police departments, as shown in Table 12.3. There did not appear to be a relationship among city police departments between agency size and type of discipline imposed for sustained complaints, except that agencies with fewer than 50 sworn personnel were slightly more likely to terminate officers than were larger agencies.

Tables B-14.2 and B-14.4 contain the information regarding disciplinary action by agency size for the county police departments and state agencies.

Table 12.1

Discipline Administered Following Sustained Complaints of Excessive Force Filed in 1991: By Agency Type

Discipline Administered	Agency Type			
	Sheriffs' Departments	County Police Departments	City Police Departments	State Agencies
Reprimand	41.9%	17.3%	32.6%	75.7%
Suspension	17.8	50.0	41.8	13.6
Reassign	4.3	5.3	0.0	1.7
Terminated	17.6	6.7	13.6	6.2
Other	18.4	20.7	12.0	2.8
Total	100.0	100.0	100.0	100

NOTE: Percentages are weighted

Table 12.2

Discipline Administered Following Sustained Excessive Force Complaints Filed in 1991: Sheriffs' Departments by Agency Size

Discipline Administered	Number of Sworn Personnel			
	1-99	100-249	250 or more	WCP*
Reprimand	9 (42.9)	8 (28.6)	12 (38.7)	41.9
Suspension	3 (14.3)	15 (53.6)	15 (48.4)	17.8
Reassign	1 (4.8)	0 (0.0)	0 (0.0)	4.3
Terminated	4 (19.0)	1 (3.6)	1 (3.2)	17.6
Other	4 (19.0)	4 (14.3)	3 (9.7)	18.4
Total Sustained Complaints	21 (100.0)	28 (100.0)	31 (100.0)	100.0
Total Responding Agencies	10	14	15	

* Weighted Column Percent

NOTE: Column totals may not sum to 100.0% due to rounding

123

Table 12.3

Discipline Administered Following Sustained Excessive Force Complaints Filed in 1991: City Police Departments by Agency Size

Discipline Administered	Number of Sworn Personnel						
	1-49	50-99	100-249	250-499	500-999	1,000 or more	WCP*
Reprimand	9 (32.1)	45 (42.1)	54 (31.0)	44 (40.7)	23 (39.7)	247 (25.9)	32.6
Suspension	12 (42.9)	24 (22.4)	68 (39.2)	28 (25.9)	20 (34.5)	578 (60.5)	41.8
Reassign	0 (0.0)	1 (0.9)	2 (1.1)	1 (0.9)	0 (0.0)	0 (0.0)	0.0
Terminated	4 (14.3)	4 (3.7)	17 (9.8)	10 (9.3)	8 (13.8)	64 (6.7)	13.6
Other	3 (10.7)	33 (30.8)	33 (19.0)	25 (23.1)	7 (12.1)	66 (6.9)	12.0
Total Sustained Complaints	28 (100.0)	107 (100.0)	174 (100.0)	108 (100.0)	58 (100.0)	955 (100.0)	100.0
Total Responding Agencies	20	34	80	32	15	13	

* Weighted Column Percent

NOTE: Column totals may not sum to 100.0% due to rounding

B.6 FACTORS ASSOCIATED WITH RECEIPT OF COMPLAINTS

As indicated in the review of the literature, a number of factors have been suggested as being associated with the likelihood that citizen complaints would be received, as well as with how those complaints would be processed. This section summarizes the results from the questionnaire concerning several of those factors.

B.6.1 SOLICITING CITIZEN COMPLAINTS

B.6.1A METHODS USED TO INFORM CITIZENS ABOUT THE COMPLAINT PROCESS

Agencies were asked to report in the survey the methods they used to inform citizens about procedures for filing complaints of police misconduct. In particular, agencies indicated whether they utilized posters, flyers, newsletters, public service announcements, or citizen complaint/ information hotlines. Responding agencies could also indicate whether they utilized "other" methods for informing citizens about procedures for filing complaints of police misconduct. These other methods included informing citizens through the phone book, newspapers, public speaking engagements by department personnel, and annual reports. Tables B-15.1 through B-15.5 summarize the agencies' responses by agency type and by agency size within agency type. Because multiple responses were possible, column percentages do not sum to 100.0 percent.

AGENCY TYPE

Greater proportions of county police departments, than the other three types of agencies, used posters and/or flyers to inform citizens about procedures for filing complaints of police misconduct. For instance, using flyers were 12.4 percent of the county police departments, 4.9 percent of the city police departments, 4.1 percent of the sheriffs' departments, and 2.3 percent of the state agencies.

More city police departments than the other three categories of agencies used newsletters to inform citizens about procedures for filing complaints of police misconduct. A relatively large proportion (27.3%) of state agencies indicated that they utilized some "other" methods than those listed for informing the citizenry about the complaint filing procedures.

AGENCY SIZE

Tables B-15.2 through B-15.5 provide the results for each agency type by agency size. Among sheriffs' departments, the size of the department, for the most part, was not associated with different frequencies of use of the various methods to inform citizens about the procedures for filing complaints of police misconduct. One exception was the use of flyers, which was more likely to be used by larger departments. One-third (29.2%) of the sheriffs' departments with 500 or more sworn personnel used flyers, compared to none of the agencies with less than 50 sworn personnel.

Among city police departments, larger departments were more likely than the smaller departments to use flyers, newsletters, public service announcements, hotlines, and "other" methods for informing citizens. For instance, whereas 32.6 percent of the city police departments with 250 or more sworn personnel used flyers, only 11.5 percent of the agencies with under 100 sworn personnel did so.

B.6.1B NUMBER OF METHODS USED TO INFORM CITIZENS ABOUT PROCEDURES FOR FILING COMPLAINTS OF POLICE MISCONDUCT

A variable was created denoting for each department the number of the above methods it used for informing citizens about procedures for filing complaints. The results are contained in Tables B-16.1 through B-16.5. Table B-16.1 prsents the weighted percentages by agency type. Tables B-16.2 through B-16.5 present the results by agency size for sheriffs' departments, county police departments, city police departments, and state agencies, respectively.

AGENCY TYPE

Sheriffs' departments were the most likely of the four types not to use any of the methods mentioned to publicize the complaint procedures. Almost three-fourths of sheriffs' agencies (72.3%) said they used none of the methods, compared to 65.9 percent of the state agencies, 62.9 percent of the county police departments, and 61.4 percent of the city police departments.

AGENCY SIZE

Among both sheriffs' and municipal departments, the smaller agencies were most likely not to use any of the methods mentioned for publicizing the complaint process. This is seen in Table B-16.2, which shows that, among sheriffs' departments, 58.4 percent of the agencies with 500 or more sworn employees used none of the methods, compared to 70.6 percent of the agencies with 1 to 24 sworn employees and 74.5 percent of the agencies with 25 to 49 sworn employees.

Table B-16.4 shows that the larger city agencies used more methods. Over seventy-five percent (75.4%) of the agencies with 500 or more sworn personnel used one or more methods compared to under 40 percent (38.5%) of the agencies with fewer than 50 sworn personnel.

Similarly, 41.4 percent of the largest agencies (1,000 or more sworn personnel) used two or more methods compared to 3.1 percent and 6.4 percent of the agencies with 1 to 24, and 25 to 49 sworn personnel, respectively.

B.6.2 COMPLAINT INTAKE PROCEDURES

B.6.2A WAYS CITIZENS CAN FILE COMPLAINTS OF POLICE MISCONDUCT

Responding departments also provided information regarding the ways that citizens can file complaints of police misconduct. That is, departments reported whether citizens might lodge complaints in person, through the mail, over the phone to the main department number, over the phone to a separate or special number (at least one of the purposes of which was to file complaints of police misconduct), or by telegram. Tables B-17.1 through B-17.5 provide the results for this inquiry. These results are described overall, by agency type, and by agency size within agency type.

AGENCY TYPE

Over 98 percent of the agencies of each type allowed a person to file a complaint in person. The remaining agencies indicated, in follow-up telephone interviews, that they required complaints to be filed through the mail.

For each of the other methods of filing, more state agencies and county police departments than sheriffs' departments and city police departments allowed citizens to file complaints in that manner. For instance, 97.7 percent of the state agencies and 99.0 percent of the county police departments allowed citizens to file complaints through the mail. By contrast, 80.1 percent of the city police departments and 85.6 percent of the sheriffs' departments allowed this method of filing. Similarly, 68.2 percent of the state agencies and 66.1 percent of the county police departments accepted complaints over a separate telephone line, compared to corresponding percentages of 41.4 and 31.0 for sheriffs' departments and city police departments, respectively.

AGENCY SIZE

Among sheriffs' departments, larger agencies were more likely than the smaller ones to allow citizens to file complaints through the mail, over the main telephone, by telegram, or over a separate telephone. For instance, 95.8 percent of the agencies with 500 or more sworn personnel allowed citizens to file complaints over the phone. In contrast, 67.3 percent of the agencies with 25 to 49 sworn personnel, and 75.0 percent of agencies with 1 to 24 sworn personnel allowed complaints to be filed in this manner.

Among city police departments, there was no apparent relationship between size and the ability of citizens to file complaints either in person or over the main telephone number. Larger departments, however, were more likely than the smaller ones to accept complaints through the mail, by telegram, or over a separate telephone line. For instance, over 95 percent (95.1%) of the agencies with 500 or more sworn personnel accepted complaints through the mail compared to only 80.4 percent of the agencies with less than 50 sworn personnel.

B.6.2B Locations Where Citizens Can File Complaints of Police Misconduct

Agencies were requested to indicate where citizens could file complaints of police misconduct. In particular, agencies were asked whether complaints could be made at agency headquarters, at district or precinct stations, at store front or mini/mobile stations, with the civil service commission, with the board of commissioners, at the civilian complaint review agency, at city hall, or at other locations. Agencies indicated as many locations as were applicable. Tables B-18.1 through B-18.5 provide these results. Some of the low percentages for certain locations (e.g., storefront or mini-stations) reflect the relatively less frequent existence of these locations among jurisdictions.

Agency Type

Virtually all of the responding agencies had provisions for citizens to file complaints of police misconduct at agency headquarters. Of the 8 agencies that did not allow for filing of complaints at agency headquarters, some had no such headquarters and the rest required filing at an alternative location such as a civilian review board office.

Not surprisingly, city police departments were more likely than any of the other three types of agencies to have citizens file complaints at city hall. Two-thirds (67.1%) of the city police departments used this location. Larger percentages of county police departments (58.6%) and state agencies (100.0%), than sheriffs' departments (12.3%) or city police departments (8.0%), reported that citizens could file complaints at district/precinct stations.

Boards of Commissioners were reported to be used for filing complaints by one-third of the sheriffs' departments (34.6%), the county police departments (36.9%), and the city police departments (30.2%). Among state law enforcement agencies, 4.5 percent said complaints could be filed with such agencies, probably reflecting the considerably different structure of such agencies.

Agency Size

As indicated in Table B-18.2, the larger sheriffs' departments were more likely than the smaller ones to allow for the filing of complaints of police misconduct at city hall, a district/ precinct station, storefront or mini-station, and/or with a civilian complaint review agency. For the most part, the smaller sheriffs' departments used agency headquarters for the filing of complaints though in more than one-third of the departments with less than 50 sworn personnel citizens were able to file complaints with a Board of Commissioners.

The largest city police departments (i.e., with 500 or more sworn personnel) were more likely than the smaller ones to accept complaints at district/precinct stations, at storefront or mini-stations, and/or at the civilian complaint review agencies. This indicates the greater physical resources (and greater geographic spread) of the larger agencies. In contrast, the smaller agencies (i.e., with fewer than 50 sworn personnel) were more likely than the larger departments to have indicated that complaints could be filed at city hall and/or with the Board of Commissioners. This information is contained in B-18.4.

Tables B-18.3 and B-18.5 contain the size information for county police departments and state agencies, respectively.

B.6.2C PERSONNEL WHO ARE AUTHORIZED TO ACCEPT COMPLAINTS FROM CITIZENS

Departments indicated who in the agency was authorized to accept complaints from citizens. That is, they indicated whether "any employee," "any sworn personnel," or "only a sworn supervisor" was authorized to accept complaints. These results are contained in Tables B-19.1 through B-19.5.

AGENCY TYPE

Over 50 percent of the sheriffs' departments (56.8%) and city police departments (62.3%) required that a supervisor accept the complaints. Another one-quarter to one-third of the agencies in each of those two categories allowed any employee to accept complaints. Approximately equal percentages of county agencies allowed only sworn supervisors to accept complaints (48.6%) or allowed any employee to accept complaints (46.9%). A majority (58.1%) of state agencies allowed any employee to receive complaints.

AGENCY SIZE

The larger sheriffs' agencies were more likely to allow any employee to accept complaints, whereas the smaller departments were more likely to require that supervisors do so. Departments of 250 to 499 and 500 or more sworn personnel, allowed for any employee to accept complaints in percentages of 40.0 and 45.8, respectively. These figures contrast with smaller departments where the percentages ranged from 18.4 to 33.3. Conversely, these smaller departments required supervisory acceptance of complaints in percentages of from 55.8 to 61.2.

Similar to sheriffs' agencies, smaller city police departments (i.e., with 249 or fewer sworn employees) were more likely to limit the acceptance of complaints to supervisors. Within the four categories denoting smaller agencies, percentages of departments that limited acceptance of complaints to supervisors ranged from 57.4 to 65.7. Conversely, the larger departments (with 250 or more sworn employees) were more likely to allow either for any employee to accept the complaints or to allow for any sworn employee to do so.

B.6.2D TIME OF DAY WHEN COMPLAINTS CAN BE FILED

Departments were asked what time of day a citizen could file a written complaint of police misconduct. These results are contained in Tables B-20.1 through B-20.5.

AGENCY TYPE

As seen in Table B-20.1, greater percentages of county police departments and state agencies, compared to sheriffs' departments and city police departments, accepted complaints at any time of day. Over 85 percent of the state agencies (93.2%) and county police departments (87.1%) accepted complaints any time of day. In contrast, three-fourths of the sheriffs' departments (72.5%) and city police departments (74.9%) accepted complaints any time of day and one-quarter of the agencies in those two types (27.0% and 23.8%, respectively) accepted complaints only during the day shift.

AGENCY SIZE

A greater percentage of the larger sheriffs' departments than smaller ones allowed for the making of a complaint at any time. For instance, 95.8 percent of the agencies with 500 or more sworn employees, compared to less than 70 percent of the agencies with fewer than 50 sworn personnel, allowed citizens to file at any time.

At least 84 percent of the city police departments, in all but one size category, allowed for the 24-hour submission of complaints. The only exception was that 69.5 percent of the agencies with fewer than 25 sworn employees allowed for 24-hour submission.

B.6.2E TIME LIMITS FOR CITIZENS TO FILE COMPLAINTS

Departments indicated whether citizens had unlimited time to file complaints regarding officer misconduct or instead, were limited to filing within one month, one to three months, three to six months, or six months up to a year after the alleged incident.

Several of the agencies of each agency type indicated that they used different time parameters than those listed in the survey for filing, or noted that the time parameters varied depending on the type of violation alleged. For instance, several departments indicated that complaints had to be filed within a "reasonable time," and several noted that alleged criminal violations had to be filed within the legal statute of limitations. These are listed as "other" in Tables B-21.1 through B-21.5 where the results from this survey item are presented.

AGENCY TYPE

All but one state agency (97.7%) allowed for complaints to be filed at any time after the alleged violation. For county police departments, sheriffs' departments, and city police departments, the corresponding percentages were 86.2, 83.2, and 81.7. Approximately 10 percent of the city police departments (11.2%), county police departments (7.9%), and sheriffs' departments (8.9%) limited citizen filing to one month.

AGENCY SIZE

Among sheriffs' departments and city police departments there was no correlation between agency size and whether there was a time limit on the filing of complaints. These results are contained in Tables B-21.2 and B-21.4.

B.6.2F TYPES OF ASSISTANCE DEPARTMENTS PROVIDE COMPLAINANTS

Departments reported the types of assistance they provided when citizens filed complaints of police misconduct. Specifically, the departments were asked whether they provided complaint forms, they provided bilingual complaint forms, officers completed the forms, civilian employees completed the forms, assistance was provided to non-English speaking citizens, copies of the complaints were provided to the citizens, the citizens were informed of the disposition of the cases (that is, they were informed as to whether the complaint was determined to be unfounded, sustained, not sustained, or the officer was exonerated), or the citizens were informed of disciplinary actions taken against officers. Multiple responses were possible. These responses are contained in Tables B-22.1 through B-22.5.

AGENCY TYPE

More county police departments (81.9%) and city police departments (63.6%) than state agencies (50.0%) and sheriffs' departments (48.8%) provided complaint forms to citizens, and more county police departments (12.0%) than the other three types of agencies provided bilingual complaint forms.

In well over a majority of county police departments (61.1%) and state agencies (75.0%), a police officer completed the complaint form. By contrast, 39.8 percent of the city police departments and 46.0 percent of the sheriffs' departments followed this practice. State agencies were more likely than the other types of agencies to allow civilian employees to complete the complaint forms.

Sheriffs' departments were least likely to assist non-English speaking complainants. Just over 50 percent (50.9%) of the sheriffs' departments reported this service, compared to 64.9 percent of the county police departments, 72.7 percent of the state agencies, and 67.1 percent of the city police departments.

Similar proportions of city police departments (56.9%), county police departments (53.9%), and sheriffs' departments (51.1%) provided copies of the complaint to the complainant. The corresponding percentage for state agencies was 27.3 percent.

At least three-fourths of the agencies within each type informed citizens of the dispositions of the complaints they had lodged. That is, they informed the citizen whether or not the complaint was sustained, not sustained, and so forth.

Approximately two-thirds of the city police departments (65.2%) and sheriffs' departments (62.6%) informed the citizen of the discipline imposed on an officer against whom a complaint was sustained. This was higher than the corresponding percentages for state agencies (47.7%) and county police departments (45.0%).

Regardless of agency type, fewer than six percent of departments said that they provided some "other" form of assistance to complainants that was not listed on the survey. Such assistance included having police officers assist in the completion of a complaint report if the complainant could not write, informing citizens of the methods of appeal, and sending letters to complainants acknowledging receipt of complaints.

AGENCY SIZE

To the extent that size is related to assistance provided to complainants, it is for the most part a positive relationship between size and the provision of services. For instance, among sheriffs' departments, size was positively related to the provision of complaint forms, provision of bilingual complaint forms, having officers complete the complaint form, assistance for non-English speaking citizens, and providing information to the complainants regarding the disposition of complaints. In contrast, the smaller agencies were more likely to inform the citizens of any disciplinary action taken.

Among city police departments the data indicated that larger departments were more likely than the smaller ones to have an officer complete the complaint form, provide bilingual complaint forms, and assist non-English speaking complainants. As with the sheriffs' departments, the smaller departments were more likely than the larger ones to inform the complainant of any disciplinary action taken against the officer.

132

B.6.2G Requirements of Citizens Filing Complaints

Law enforcement agencies responding to the survey indicated whether or not a person submitting a complaint of police misconduct had to sign the complaint, swear to the complaint, certify the complaint, or notarize the complaint. Multiple responses were possible. These results are contained in Tables B-23.1 through B-23.5.

Agency Type

As seen in Table B-23.1, between one-half and three-fourths of the agencies within each type required the complainant to sign the complaint. This included 78.5 percent of the city police departments, 76.3 percent of the sheriffs' departments, 64.3 percent of the county police departments, and 52.3 percent of the state agencies.

Sheriffs' departments were most likely, and state agencies least likely, to require that citizens swear to the complaints. In descending order, the percentage of departments requiring citizens to swear to the complaints were 32.0 percent of sheriffs' departments, 23.9 percent of city police departments, 17.3 percent of county police departments, and 9.1 percent of state agencies.

Between 5 and 15 percent of the departments within each category required that complaints be certified and between 16 and 19 percent of the sheriffs' departments, county police departments, and city police departments required notarization. Just 4.5 percent of the state agencies required notarization of complaints.

Agency Size

For the most part, the requirements of the complaints did not vary with the size of the sheriffs' departments. The one notable exception was that the smaller departments (with fewer than 250 sworn personnel) were more likely than the larger departments to require that the citizens sign the complaints.

As with sheriffs' agencies, the only notable difference among city police departments of various sizes was that smaller agencies were more likely to require signatures on the complaints than were the larger departments.

B.6.3 COMPLAINT INVESTIGATIONS

B.6.3A EXISTENCE OF A CIVILIAN COMPLAINT REVIEW AGENCY

Agencies were requested to indicate whether their jurisdiction had a civilian complaint review board or agency. The results are contained in Tables B-24.1 through B-24.5.

AGENCY TYPE

Between 4 and 12 percent of agencies of each type indicated their jurisdictions had civilian complaint review boards. Civilian review boards were reported by 11.4 percent of the county departments, 7.0 percent of the sheriffs' departments, 5.3 percent of the city police departments, and 4.4 percent of state agencies.

AGENCY SIZE

Among sheriffs' departments, there was no relationship between agency size and having such boards. Approximately 8 percent of both the agencies with 500 or more sworn personnel (8.3%) and with one to 24 sworn personnel (7.7%) had civilian review boards.

Among municipal departments, larger agencies were much more likely to have civilian review boards. Among agencies with 1,000 or more sworn personnel, 58.6 percent indicated that they had such boards; among those with between 500 and 999 officers, 37.5 percent had civilian review agencies. The percentage with such units was approximately 5 percent in the smallest agencies.

B.6.3B PERSONS OR UNITS WHO CONDUCT ADMINISTRATIVE INVESTIGATIONS OF CITIZEN COMPLAINTS OF POLICE USE OF EXCESSIVE FORCE

Agencies responding to the survey indicated which categories of personnel conducted administrative (non-criminal) investigations of citizen complaints alleging police use of excessive force. That is, they indicated whether these reviews were conducted by sworn personnel, non-sworn personnel, the Internal Affairs Unit, a civilian complaint review board, the Office of Professional Standards, or some other person or entity. Multiple responses were possible. These results are contained in Tables B-25.1 through B-25.5.

AGENCY TYPE

At least two-thirds of the agencies in each category indicated that sworn personnel conducted investigations of citizen complaints. Investigations by sworn officers were reported by 77.8 percent of the state agencies, 67.3 percent of the county police departments, 66.9 percent of the city police departments, and 66.1 percent of the sheriffs' departments.

Investigations of civilian complaints by non-sworn personnel was mentioned by similar proportions of agencies within each type. This included 5.0 percent of sheriffs' departments, 3.3 percent of city police departments, 2.5 percent of county police departments, and no state agencies.

Internal Affairs units were said to conduct investigations of complaints most often among state agencies (77.8%) and county police departments (70.2%). Internal Affairs units were used for this purpose in 18.9 percent of the sheriffs' departments and 13.1 percent of the city police departments.

Similar percentages of county police departments (5.3%), city departments (4.0%), and sheriffs' departments (4.2%) reported that civilian complaint review boards investigated complaints. None of the responding state agencies indicated that civilian boards investigated civilian complaints.

Investigations by an Office of Professional Standards was most often mentioned by state agencies (20.0%), followed by county police departments (8.0%), sheriffs' departments (3.8%), and city police departments (3.1%).

Between 6 and 39 percent of the agencies within each category indicated some entity "other" than those listed, conducted the investigation of complaints. These included the assistant chief, chief, use of force review board, state's attorney, or district attorney.

AGENCY SIZE

Among sheriffs' departments, larger agencies were more likely to have used specialized units such as Internal Affairs and Office of Professional Standards to investigate citizen complaints. Smaller agencies were more likely to have "other" persons conducting the investigations.

Among municipal departments, larger agencies were much more likely to have complaints investigated by Internal Affairs units, civilian review boards, Offices of Professional Standards, and non-sworn personnel. Smaller agencies were more likely to have investigations conducted by "other" persons.

B.6.3C How the Internal Affairs Function is Handled

Responding departments provided information on the way in which the internal affairs function was handled. Specifically, they indicated in which of the following three ways the function was handled:

1) Internal Affairs division or unit with full-time responsibility existed,
2) Cases were formally assigned to specific individuals, or
3) Complaints were handled on a case-by-case basis.

These results are contained in Tables B-26.1 through B-26.5.

Agency Type

State agencies, followed by county police departments, were the most likely to indicate that their internal affairs function was handled by a full-time Internal Affairs (IA) unit. Among state agencies, 82.2 percent had IA units, 11.1 percent assigned on a case-by-case basis, and 6.7 percent formally assigned cases to individuals for handling.

Sixty-eight (67.6%) of the county agencies had full-time Internal Affairs units. Twenty-one percent (20.5%) handled the function on a case-by-case manner, and another 11.9 percent handled cases by assigning them to particular individuals.

In two-thirds (69.3%) of the sheriffs' departments, internal affairs was handled on a case-by-case basis. Just under twenty percent (19.2%) formally assigned cases to individuals, and 11.5 percent used full-time Internal Affairs units.

Similar to sheriffs' departments, two-thirds (64.1%) of the city agencies handled internal affairs on a case by case basis and just under 30 percent (28.9%) assigned cases to particular individuals for handling. Seven percent (7.1%) had full-time Internal Affairs units.

Agency Size

Larger departments were the most likely to have full-time IA divisions. Among sheriffs' agencies, for example, 95.8 percent of the agencies with 500 or more sworn personnel had IA units, as did 96.8 percent of the agencies with 250 to 499 sworn personnel. None of the agencies of this size handled complaints on a case-by-case basis. In contrast, within the three categories denoting the smallest agencies (1 to 24 sworn personnel, 25 to 49 sworn personnel, and 50 to 99 sworn personnel), zero, 17.0, and 19.5 percent had IA units. Between 50 and 84 percent of these agencies handled cases on a case-by-case basis.

All of the city police departments with 250 or more sworn personnel assigned complaints to full-time IA units, as did 68.6 percent of the city agencies with 100 to 249 sworn personnel. Agencies with fewer than 100 sworn officers were more likely to handle such complaints on a case-by-case basis or to assign them to a particular individual.

B.6.3D Rank of the Head of Internal Affairs

Overall, 46.0 percent of the law enforcement agencies that responded to the survey had full-time Internal Affairs Units. As an indication of the importance given to those units, these agencies were asked to provide the rank of the individual in charge of this unit. This information is contained in Tables B-27.1 through B-27.5. The percentages in these tables are not weighted by size because they apply to a non-random sub-sample whose underlying distribution among all agencies is not known. Therefore, these results should not be generalized beyond the particular sample under analysis.

Agency Type

Among sheriffs' agencies with IA units, the person in charge of those units had the rank of lieutenant or above 69.6 percent of the time.

Among county police departments, those in charge of the IA units had the rank of lieutenant or above in 83.3 percent of the cases.

Among municipal police departments with Internal Affairs units, 71.4 percent of those units were headed by someone with the rank of lieutenant or above.

State agencies with IA units indicated that in 80.1 percent of those agencies the units were headed by someone with the rank of lieutenant or above.

Agency Size

In general, the larger the department, the higher the rank of the person in charge of the Internal Affairs unit. Among sheriffs' departments, for example, 94.2 percent of the agencies with IA units and 250 or more sworn personnel had heads of their IA units of the rank of lieutenant or higher. Among agencies with fewer than 250 sworn officers, however, the comparable figure was 52.4 percent.

Among city police departments with Internal Affairs units and 250 or more sworn officers, 75.8 percent had heads of those agencies of the rank of lieutenant or higher. Among agencies with fewer than 250 officers, 66.2 percent had IA units headed by persons of that rank or higher.

B.6.3E Department Policies Regarding the Review of Citizen Complaints Outside the Chain of Command Where the Officer is Assigned

Another indication of the attention paid to investigations of citizen complaints of excessive force is whether the department requires that a complaint be reviewed *outside* the chain of command of the officer against whom that complaint is filed. The survey findings pertaining to this practice are contained in Tables B-28.1 through B-28.5.

AGENCY TYPE

More county police departments and state agencies than sheriffs' departments and city police departments had policies that required review of citizen complaints outside the charged officer's chain of command. Fifty percent (50.0%) of the county police departments and 43.2 percent of the state agencies had such a policy, compared to 19.0 percent each of the sheriffs' and city police departments.

AGENCY SIZE

Among sheriffs' departments, larger agencies were more likely to require that a review be handled outside the officer's chain of command. One half of the agencies with 500 or more sworn officers had such a requirement, compared to 19 percent among those with fewer than 50 officers.

A similar pattern was found among city police departments. Over sixty-five percent of the departments with more than 500 sworn officers required outside reviews of complaints, compared to approximately 20 percent of those with fewer than 50 officers.

B.6.3F TIME LIMITS FOR COMPLETING INVESTIGATIONS OF CITIZEN COMPLAINTS

Departments indicated in the survey the time allowed for the completion of investigations of citizen complaints against departmental personnel. Responding agencies indicated whether there was no time limit or limits of "within one month," "1 month up to 3 months," "3 months up to 6 months," "6 months up to one year," or some "other" time limit. These results are provided in Tables B-29.1 through B-29.5.

AGENCY TYPE

State agencies were the least likely to indicate that they had no time limits for the investigation of complaints. Forty-seven percent (46.7%) of those departments reported having no time limit, compared to 58.9 percent of county police departments, 62.2 percent of city police departments, and 67.1 percent of sheriffs' departments.

One third of the state agencies indicated that their time limit for investigating complaints was "within one month," and another 13.3 percent indicated that the time limits for completing investigations was between one and three months.

One-quarter of the other three types of agencies had time limits of one month for completing investigations, and between 5 and 15 percent of the agencies within each type had time limits of one month to three months.

Between 0 and 5 percent of the agencies within each type indicated they had a limit that did not fit one of the stated categories (indicated in the tables as "other"), such as "on a case by case basis," "as long as necessary," "as soon as possible," and "at the chief's discretion."

AGENCY SIZE

Among sheriffs' departments, smaller agencies were more likely than larger ones to have no time limit on the completion of investigations of citizen complaints. Among sheriffs' departments with 1 to 24 sworn personnel, for example, 66.7 percent had no time limit on these investigations, compared to 29.2 percent of those with 500 or more sworn officers.

Among city police departments, the same pattern held; smaller departments were more likely to have no time limits on the investigations of complaints. Among departments with fewer than 50 officers, for example, over 60 percent had no time limits, compared to 27.6 percent of those with 1,000 or more officers.

B.6.3G POLICIES REGARDING THE ABILITY OF AN OFFICER AGAINST WHOM A COMPLAINT HAS BEEN FILED TO REFUSE, WITHOUT PENALTY, TO PROVIDE INFORMATION DURING THE INVESTIGATION

In order to better determine the nature of the investigations conducted in response to citizen complaints of excessive force, agencies were asked if the officers against whom complaints were filed could refuse to provide information to the investigators without suffering negative consequences. The results are contained in Tables B-30.1 through B-30.5.

AGENCY TYPE

More sheriffs' departments and city police departments allowed their officers to refuse to provide information during investigations of citizen complaints. Twenty-eight (28.2%) of the sheriffs' departments, 27.3 percent of the city police departments, 13.0 percent of the county police departments, and 4.5 percent of the state agencies gave officers this option.

AGENCY SIZE

Among sheriffs' departments and city police departments, the smaller agencies were much more likely to allow officers to refuse to provide information than the larger agencies. Thirty-seven percent (36.7%) of the sheriffs' agencies with 1 to 24 sworn personnel, and 17.8 percent of the sheriffs' agencies with 25 to 49 sworn personnel, gave officers this option. In contrast, none of the sheriffs' agencies with 500 or more sworn personnel allowed officers not to provide information.

Among city agencies with fewer than 50 sworn officers, 22.9 percent gave officers the option of refusing to provide information without negative consequences. On the other hand, among agencies with more than 250 officers, approximately 3 percent allowed officers to withhold information.

B.6.4   DISPOSITION DECISIONS

B.6.4A PERSONS OR UNITS WHO REVIEW THE INVESTIGATIVE REPORTS AND MAKE RECOMMENDATIONS

Each agency was asked to indicate who reviewed the investigative reports and made recommendations for disciplinary action in cases involving allegations of excessive force. In particular, agencies were asked whether a review was made by the immediate supervisor, a mid-level supervisor, a high-level administrator, the chief executive of the agency, the Internal Affairs unit, a civilian complaint review agency, a Board of Police Commissioners, or someone else. Multiple responses were possible. Table B-31.1 indicates the weighted percentage of departments within each type of agency that received recommendations for disciplinary action from each category of personnel. Tables B-31.2 through B-31.5 provide the corresponding information for each agency type by agency size.

AGENCY TYPE

Sheriffs' departments, county police departments and city police departments provided similar responses concerning the persons who reviewed investigative reports and made recommendations. Over 80 percent of all three types reported that the top executive officer (e.g., chief, commissioner, sheriff) reviewed the investigative report and recommended disciplinary action. A lower percentage of state agencies (62.2%) than the other types of agencies had the top executive officer review the complaint investigative reports and make recommendations regarding disciplinary action. This finding perhaps reflects the greater decentralization of state agencies.

Conversely, state agencies were more likely than the other types to report that immediate supervisors were responsible for reviewing investigative reports and making recommendations. Among state agencies, 57.8 percent indicated that immediate supervisors played this role, compared to approximately one-third of the agencies of the other three types.

County police departments and state agencies were more likely than sheriffs' departments and city police departments to use Internal Affairs units to review investigations and recommend disciplinary action. Forty-five percent (44.7%) of the county police departments and 40.0 percent of the state agencies, compared to 10.2 percent of the sheriffs' departments and 8.0 percent of the city police departments had Internal Affairs perform this function.

Between 10 and 34 percent of the agencies within each type indicated that reviews of investigative reports and recommendations for disciplinary action were made by someone other than those persons or entities mentioned on the questionnaire. Included among those persons or entities were review committees, division commanders, legal counsels, administrative hearing boards, city attorneys, district attorneys, and various other entities.

AGENCY SIZE

Among sheriffs' departments, as shown in Table B-31.2, smaller agencies were much more likely than larger ones to have the top executive officer review the complaint investigative report. Larger agencies were somewhat more likely to have the report reviewed by an Internal Affairs unit.

Larger city police departments were more likely to have investigative reports reviewed by an Internal Affairs unit and less likely to have them reviewed by the chief. The largest agencies (1,000 or more sworn personnel) were most likely to have a civilian review board or agency review the report and make recommend-ations for disciplinary action.

B.6.4B PERSON OR UNIT WITH FINAL RESPONSIBILITY FOR ACTING ON THE RECOMMENDATIONS FOR DISCIPLINARY ACTION

Each agency was asked to indicate which person or unit had final responsibility for acting on the recommendations for disciplinary action for the use of excessive force. In particular, agencies were asked whether final authority lay with the chief executive of the agency, the city or county manager, a board of police commissioners, the mayor or other elected official, or someone else. These results are contained in Tables B-32.1 through B-32.5.

AGENCY TYPE

More sheriffs' departments (90.4%) and county police departments (94.2%) than the other agency types placed final responsibility for acting on the recommendations for disciplinary action with the agency head (i.e., sheriff, chief). By comparison, the head of the agency had final responsibility for acting on the recommendations in 77.8 percent of the state agencies and 56.0 percent of the city police departments.

City police departments, more than the other types of agencies, placed final responsibility for acting on recommendations for disciplinary action with the city/county manager (6.8%), or with the mayor or other elected official (21.8%). This appears to reflect the differential accountability structure of municipal agencies compared to the other types.

Between 3 and 12 percent of the agencies within each type indicated that another person or office not listed on the survey had the final responsibility for acting on the recommendations for disciplinary action in the use of excessive force. These "other" entities included county prosecutors, public safety directors, district attorneys, merit boards, and other such positions.

AGENCY SIZE

Among sheriffs' departments, there was no apparent relationship between agency size and the status of the person who had final responsibility for acting on recommendations for disciplinary action, except that just two-thirds (66.7%) of the agencies with 1,000 or more sworn personnel gave the sheriff final responsibility for acting on recommendations for disciplinary action, compared to around 90 percent of the agencies within the other size categories.

A majority of the city police departments, in all size categories, placed final responsibility for discipline with the chief or commissioner. The smallest city police departments were more likely than the larger ones to give final responsibility for discipline to a Board of Police Commissioners or to the mayor. With regard to the latter, one-fourth (25.8%) of the agencies with 1 to 24 sworn personnel gave the mayor this responsibility, compared to no more than 9.2 percent of the agencies in the other size categories. The largest departments, with 1,000 or more sworn personnel, were more likely to place this responsibility with trial boards or with civilian complaint review boards.

B.6.5 FOLLOW-UP

B.6.5A POLICIES REGARDING APPEALS

Agencies were requested to indicate who had the right to appeal a decision concerning disciplinary action involving alleged excessive force: no one, both the citizen and the police officer, only the citizen, or only the officer. These results are contained in Tables B-33.1 through B-33.5.

AGENCY TYPE

Overall, more than 90 percent of the agencies of each type allowed officers to appeal a decision concerning complaints of misconduct. Ninety-seven percent of the county police departments (97.4%) and city police departments (97.1%) allowed for this, as well as 95.4 percent of the state agencies and 92.3 percent of the sheriffs' departments.

Large majorities of city police departments (75.4%) and sheriffs' departments (70.0%) allowed for citizens to appeal, as well. Slightly over half (50.4 percent) of county police departments allowed such appeals, compared to 38.6 percent of state agencies. (Two city departments indicated that only the citizen could appeal.)

AGENCY SIZE

Among sheriffs' departments, larger agencies were much less likely than smaller ones to allow both the citizen and the officer to appeal decisions concerning citizen complaints. Among agencies with fewer than 25 sworn officers, for example, 74.0 percent allowed both parties to appeal, compared to 20.8 percent of the agencies with 500 or more sworn personnel. On the other hand, larger agencies were much more likely to allow appeals only by the accused officer. Thus, among agencies with fewer than 25 sworn officers, 18.0 percent allowed for appeals only by the officer, compared to 75.0 percent among agencies with 500 or more sworn personnel.

A similar, although less striking, pattern was found among city police departments, with larger agencies less likely to allow appeals by both civilians and officers, but rather, more likely to allow appeals only by the accused officer. Among departments with 500 or more sworn officers, for example 41.4 percent allowed appeals by both parties, compared to 79.4 percent of the departments with fewer than 25 officers. By contrast, 40.0 percent of the agencies with 500 or more sworn personnel allowed appeals only by officers, compared to 17.5 percent of the departments with fewer than 25 officers.

B.6.5B COUNSELING FOR OFFICERS IDENTIFIED AS USING EXCESSIVE FORCE

Responding departments were asked to indicate whether counseling was mandatory, optional, or not provided to officers identified as using excessive force. Responses are summarized in Tables B-34.1 through B-34.5

AGENCY TYPE

More county police departments, compared to the other types of agencies, indicated that counseling was mandatory for officers identified as using excessive force. Just under 56 percent (55.6%) of these agencies indicated that counseling was mandatory, compared to 40.0 percent or less of the other agency types. State agencies (51.2%) were more likely to make counseling optional, and sheriffs' departments, more than the other types of agencies, did not provide counseling (40.8%) for these types of situations.

AGENCY SIZE

The larger sheriffs' departments (i.e., with 250 or more sworn personnel) were more likely to mandate counseling for officers identified as using excessive force; the smaller departments (i.e., with fewer than 100 sworn personnel) were more likely not to provide such counseling at all.

Between 35 and 44 percent of the city agencies in each of the seven size categories mandated counseling for officers identified as using excessive force. Larger departments, however, were more likely to provide optional counseling and smaller departments were least likely to make counseling available.

B.6.5C RETRAINING FOR OFFICERS IDENTIFIED AS USING EXCESSIVE FORCE

Supplementing the question regarding the provision of counseling was another asking departments to indicate whether retraining was mandatory or optional or not provided to officers identified as using excessive force. These results are contained in Tables B-35.1 through B-35.5.

AGENCY TYPE

As with the provision of counseling, more county police departments than the other types of departments mandated retraining for this group of officers. Fifty-seven percent (57.1%) of the county police departments mandated retraining, compared to 44.2 percent of the state agencies, 36.2 percent of the city police departments, and 35.3 percent of the sheriffs' departments.

Slightly less than three percent (2.3%) of state agencies did not provide either mandatory or optional retraining for officers identified as using excessive force. This contrasts with the corresponding percentages in the other agency types of 42.3, 31.9, and 15.6 for sheriffs' departments, city police departments, and county police departments, respectively, which did not provide retraining.

AGENCY SIZE

A greater proportion of the largest sheriffs' departments (with 500 or more sworn personnel), compared to smaller ones, required retraining for officers identified as using excessive force. Conversely, a greater percentage of the smallest agencies (i.e., with fewer than 250 sworn personnel), compared to the larger ones, did not provide retraining at all to identified officers. For example, over one-half (52.3%) of the agencies with 1 to 24 sworn personnel, and 21.1 percent of the agencies with 25 to 49 sworn personnel, did not provide retraining to officers identified as misusing force. In comparison, the corresponding percentage for the agencies with 500 or more sworn personnel was 8.3.

Among city police departments, there was no relationship indicated between agency size and mandated retraining of officers identified as using excessive force. Optional retraining, however, was provided by a greater proportion of the largest agencies (500 or more sworn personnel) and, conversely, more of the smaller agencies (with fewer than 50 sworn personnel) did not provide this type of retraining at all.

B.6.5D DEPARTMENT PUBLICATION OF SUMMARY INFORMATION ON INVESTIGATIONS OF POLICE MISCONDUCT

Agencies were asked whether they published summary information concerning investigations of citizens' complaints of police misconduct for dissemination to the public. These results are contained in Tables B-36.1 through B-36.5. Weighted percentages are provided for sheriffs' departments, county police departments, and city police departments.

AGENCY TYPE

Publishing of summary information on investigations of misconduct was most common among county police departments; 45.8 percent of those agencies indicated that they published such information. Twenty-two percent (22.2%) of the state departments published this information, compared to 12.3 percent of the city police departments and 9.3 percent of the sheriffs' departments.

AGENCY SIZE

Among sheriffs' departments, larger agencies were much more likely than smaller ones to publish information about investigations of misconduct. Over 40 percent (41.8%) of the agencies with 250 or more sworn officers said they published such information. By contrast, 10.1 percent of the sheriffs departments with fewer than 250 sworn personnel did so.

As with sheriffs' departments, large city police departments were more likely to publish summary information than were small ones. Among departments with 500 or more sworn officers, 46.7 percent published such information. Among departments with fewer than 500 sworn officers, however, 21.0 percent published such information.

C. CIVIL SUITS AND CRIMINAL CHARGES

To provide a better understanding of the legal and financial consequences of allegations of excessive force, the surveyed agencies were asked to provide information concerning the number of civil suits and criminal charges alleging use of excessive force, the disposition of those suits and charges, and the amount paid in civil litigation cases in which damages were awarded to the plaintiff.

The reliability and validity of these data are affected by the varying definitions used by departments, as well as by the various methods used to collect this information. Further, as discussed more thoroughly below, a significant number of agencies which returned surveys did not provide the information requested regarding civil suits and criminal charges. Thus, interpretation of these data must be made with the recognition that to the extent that the responding agencies may not be representative of law enforcement agencies in general, the estimates themselves may not be representative.

C.1 Number of Civil Suits and Criminal Charges

A total of 329 responding agencies provided data concerning civil suits resulting from allegations of excessive force by police officers in 1991. As shown in Table B-37, data were provided by 71 sheriffs' agencies, 17 county police departments, 219 city police departments, and 22 state agencies. The limited number of agencies supplying data was largely attributable to the fact, as explained on a number of questionnaires and in follow-up interviews, that many departments did not keep information concerning civil suits. Instead, such data were maintained by the city attorney or some other outside entity. In addition, several agencies indicated that they were unable or unwilling to release such information, out of concern that it might prove to be politically controversial or would provoke additional inquiries from litigants.

The 329 agencies that provided data reported a total of 2,558 civil suits that had resulted in 1991 from charges of excessive force. Of those, as Table B-37 also shows, 415 were reported by sheriffs' departments, 94 by county police departments, 1,886 by city police departments, and 163 by state law enforcement agencies.

As is also shown in Table B-37, information concerning criminal charges was provided by 348 agencies, including 73 sheriffs' departments, 17 county police departments, 236 city police departments, and 22 state agencies.

The responding agencies supplied information concerning a total of 122 criminal charges alleging excessive force in 1991, 14 involving sheriffs' departments, 4 involving county police departments, 100 involving city police departments, and 4 involving state agencies.

C.2 Rates of Civil Suits and Criminal Charges

To standardize the data concerning the number of civil suits and criminal charges reported in 1991, rates per 1,000 sworn officers were created in the same fashion as those previously discussed concerning incidents of use of force and numbers of citizen complaints.

Tables B-38.1 through B-38.5 contain the rates of civil suits and criminal charges for each agency type, by size categories. Because of the small number of agencies providing data, and the fact that the responses are from a non-random subset of the total sample, weighting to produce overall adjusted agency rates was not appropriate. As a result, all comparisons will be limited to those across agency sizes, within the same agency type.

As shown in Table B-38.2, the highest rates of civil suits alleging excessive force among sheriffs' departments were found among the smallest agencies, with those rates declining consistently before increasing among agencies with 1,000 or more sworn officers. Because of the extremely small numbers of agencies providing data, however, these results must be treated only as suggestive. No pattern was apparent across agency size with respect to rates of criminal charges.

Among county police departments, the rates of civil suits demonstrated a pattern similar to that found among sheriffs' agencies; again, the extremely small numbers of departments providing data make these results tenuous. No pattern was found across agency sizes with respect to rates of criminal charges.

Rates of civil suits reported by city police departments were highest among the smallest and the largest agencies. The highest rate of criminal charges was reported among agencies with fewer than 25 sworn officers. The small number of agencies providing information precludes generalizing from these findings to the larger sample.

The number of state agencies providing information was too small to permit valid comparisons across agency sizes.

C.3 RESOLUTION OF CIVIL SUITS

Tables B-39.1 through B-39.5 provide information concerning the resolution of civil suits alleging excessive use of force that were reported by agencies responding to the national survey. Table 39.1 provides the resolution of suits by agency type. Because the data were provided by a small, non-random subset of the overall sample, these figures have not been weighted according to agency size. As a result, they are heavily influenced by the data provided by the largest departments. Interpretation of these results, therefore, should be undertaken in conjunction with an awareness of the distribution of cases by agency size as shown in Tables B-39.2 through B-39.5.

AGENCY TYPE

Regardless of agency type, approximately two-thirds of the civil suits alleging excessive force filed in 1991 were still pending when the survey was completed. The only notable difference across agency types was that the percent of suits filed against state agencies that were settled out of court (3.1%) was lower than the percent settled out of court among sheriffs' departments (17.3%), city police departments (19.2 percent), and county police departments (26.0%). The percentage of suits settled in favor of litigants ranged from 5.0 percent among state agencies, to 8.8 percent among sheriffs' departments, to 9.5 percent among city police departments, to 16.0 percent among county police departments.

AGENCY SIZE

As Tables 39.2 through 39.5 indicate, no clear differences in resolution of civil suits were apparent by agency size, regardless of agency type.

C.4 AMOUNTS PAID IN CIVIL CASES FINDING EXCESSIVE FORCE

Tables B-40.1 and B-40.2 provide information about the amounts paid in 1991 in civil litigation cases alleging excessive use of force. As with the above analyses, weighting of responses by agency size in Table B-40.1 was inappropriate. Thus, the results generally overrepresent cases in larger agencies. The breakdown of amounts paid by agency size are provided in Table B-40.2.

Although the small number of cases makes rigorous comparisons inappropriate, certain general findings are worth noting. For example, the 24 sheriffs' departments that reported civil litigation resulting in awards to the litigant paid over $3.5 million in 33 cases. Among the 72 city police departments reporting awards, they paid almost $45 million in awards in 79 cases. The amounts paid per case ranged widely, up to over $565,000 among the 79 cases reported by city departments.

C.5 RESOLUTION OF CRIMINAL CHARGES

Departments were also asked to provide information concerning the resolutions of the criminal cases that resulted from excessive force complaints filed in 1991. The results of the analyses of these responses are contained in Tables B-41.1 through B-41.5. Again, weighting by agency size was inappropriate.

AGENCY TYPE

Although there were too few criminal cases reported by county police departments and state agencies to make meaningful analysis possible, it is worth noting that among sheriffs' agencies and city departments, approximately one-quarter of the cases were still pending at the time of the survey. Among both those types of agencies, slightly less than 60 percent of the cases had been settled in favor of the defendant.

AGENCY SIZE

No clear patterns emerged across agency sizes in terms of the resolution of criminal charges.

V. SUMMARY AND DISCUSSION

The legitimate use of coercive force is the critical factor distinguishing policing from all other professions. In fact, because many of the objectives of police officers must be achieved over the objections of others, as in making an arrest or separating the participants in a brawl, police must be able to utilize force. Unfortunately, however, the general public is usually made aware of the police use of force only on those occasions when the use of such force is, or appears to be, excessive.

Despite the central importance of the use of force to the police role, there has been relatively little empirical research conducted concerning the extent and rate per officer of the use of such force, how the use of force varies across agencies, the extent and rate of citizen complaints of excessive force, the disposition of those complaints, the frequency of civil and criminal litigation pertaining to excessive force, and the various factors that may affect both the use of force and complaints of excessive force.

Recognizing the need for further research on these issues, the National Institute of Justice provided support to the Police Foundation to conduct a comprehensive national survey of law enforcement agencies to address them.

A total of 1,111 law enforcement agencies completed the extensive questionnaire used in this study. This report has presented a review of the existing literature on the use of force by police, described the methods by which the survey was conducted, and presented the major results. This final chapter provides a summary of the report and a brief discussion of its implications.

A. PRIOR LITERATURE ON THE USE OF FORCE

An extensive review of existing literature on the use of force by police revealed that most of the research on force has focused narrowly on police use of deadly force, and all but a handful of studies have focused on only one or a few, mostly urban, jurisdictions. Nonetheless, that previous work was valuable in providing a framework for the national survey of law enforcement agencies that is the focus of this report.

A.1 USE OF FORCE

The limited available empirical research indicates that police officers use force infrequently. Researchers have utilized departmental use of force data, observations of police, citizen surveys, and surveys of law enforcement personnel to gauge the extent to which force is used. Among observational studies, the frequency of force is said to occur in between 1.05 (Worden, 1992) and 5.1 (Reiss, 1971; Friedrich, 1980) percent of police-citizen encounters. Excessive force is reportedly used in between one-third of one percent (Worden, 1992) and 1.8 percent (Reiss, 1972; Friedrich, 1980) of the encounters. One citizen survey (Whitaker, 1982) found that 13.6 percent of respondents perceived themselves to have been victims of police misconduct, including excessive force.

A.2 DEPARTMENTAL POLICIES AND PRACTICES TO REDUCE FORCE

Some of the research has attempted to relate the nature and extent of force to departmental policies and practices. In general, that research has found that force levels vary with the restrictiveness of written policy and with the extent to which compliance with restrictive policies is promoted by the administration (e.g., Uelman, 1973; Fyfe, 1978).

In addition to adopting and enforcing restrictive policies, some law enforcement agencies are attempting to screen out, at the hiring stage, those persons who are inclined toward excessive or unnecessary force. As such, some research has attempted to identify characteristics of officers who use force frequently (e.g., Croft, 1985) or force excessively (e.g., Worden, 1992). Some characteristics which have been associated with low force use are age, experience, education, and African American origin. Several researchers (e.g., Black and Reiss, 1967 and Worden, 1992) have associated use of force with certain negative, narrow, or prejudiced attitudes of officers.

Training to reduce force has taken several forms, including increasing the emphases on verbal skills. Researchers have evaluated these interventions and found mixed results (e.g., Fyfe, 1987; Toch, Grant and Galvin, 1975). Another force reduction strategy is to identify in-service officers prone to use force and intervene with ameliorative strategies. These monitoring interventions, too, have produced mixed results (e.g., Smith, 1974; Broadaway, 1974).

A.3 CITIZEN COMPLAINTS OF EXCESSIVE FORCE

There has been a limited amount of research designed to determine the extent to which police activity generates citizen complaints of misconduct. The New York City Civilian Complaint Review Board (1990), for example, determined that one to five complaints of police misconduct are generated for every 10,000 police-citizen encounters. Dugan and Breda (1991), using data from 165 Washington state agencies, found that complaints numbered .27 per year per "public-contact enforcement officer in the agency" (p. 166).

Excessive force complaints are usually a small proportion of the types of complaints received, comprising between 15 and 35 percent of all complaints of police misconduct (e.g., Perez, 1978; Duga and Breda, 1991).

Several commentators have conjectured that high rates of complaints may reflect citizen confidence in and awareness of the complaint process (West, 1988; Walker and Bumphus, 1992). This has been supported by several case studies where the adoption of new, more receptive, complaint receipt and processing procedures have been followed by dramatic increases in the number of complaints filed (e.g., Kahn, 1975; Littlejohn, 1981).

In some cases, new complaint procedures have incorporated civilian review of complaints. In a number of cities these entities were adopted because the public had lost faith in the internal systems. Walker and Bumphus (1992) recently reported that just under 70 percent of the 50 largest cities have some sort of civilian review. West's (1988) findings have indicated, however, that this percentage does not apply to the smaller cities.

Other procedures which might encourage complaints or increase the likelihood of fair scrutiny pertain to the intake and investigation processes. Some case studies have indicated that intake procedures in some departments create obstacles for citizens that discourage complaints or lead to their withdrawal. Other researchers (e.g., Berel and Sisk, 1964, and Broadaway, 1974) have surveyed multiple departments about their intake procedures. According to these studies, the "normal practice" is for departments to accept complaints 24-hours per day, seven days per week, either in person, by mail, or by phone, and to accept anonymous complaints. Complaints in person could be lodged at several departmental locations. A number of departments, however, require in-person filings, or notarization of the complaint report, or both.

In terms of the investigation of complaints, some prior research indicates that Internal Affairs Units are usually the departmental entity charged with this stage of the process (New York City Civilian Review Board, 1986; West, 1988), though less serious complaints might be handled within the officers' divisions. One common problem for the investigators is the lack of objective eye witnesses. Kerstetter and Van Winkle (1989) determined that 40 percent of the complaints in one city had witnesses, but that only 28 percent of these witnesses were "independent," that is they were neither a police officer nor related to or involved with the complainant.

Some researchers have related the lack of witnesses to the low percentage of complaint dispositions that are sustained (e.g., Weitzer, 1986). Various studies have found that complaints of police misconduct are sustained at rates of between zero (Culver, 1975) and 25 percent (Dugan and Breda, 1991), and that, generally, excessive force complaints are sustained at a lower level than other types of complaints (e.g., Wagner, 1980; Dugan and Breda, 1991). In addition to presence of witnesses (Weitzer, 1986), researchers have linked rates of sustained complaints to such factors as the number of complaints received (West, 1988; Walker and Bumphus, 1992), the type of review system used (Perez, 1978), the characteristics of persons who lodge the complaints, and the departmental commitment to fair review (St. Clair, 1992).

Research has determined that sustained complaints usually result in either reprimands or suspensions (see e.g., Culver, 1975), rather than dismissals. Some of the case studies of departments have determined that discipline has been "lax" (e.g., Independent Commission on the Los Angeles Police Department, 1991; Kolts, 1992).

B.   THE POLICE FOUNDATION STUDY

B.1 THE LAW ENFORCEMENT AGENCY SURVEY

Although a number of researchers have addressed issues of police use of force, complaints of excessive force, and related topics, much remains to be learned. To address this need, the Police Foundation received funding from the National Institute of Justice to conduct a survey of a representative national sample of law enforcement agencies using a questionnaire designed to elicit information pertaining to many of the issues identified in the literature review. After several revisions, a draft version of a questionnaire was subjected to pre-testing, additional revision, and approval by staff of the National Institute of Justice.

The final instrument was distributed to a stratified random sample of 1,697 agencies. The initial mailing of the questionnaire occurred in mid-August of 1992. After repeated remailings and recontacts, a total of 1,111 completed questionnaires were received, coded, and placed into computer-readable format. These responding agencies produced a response rate of 67.2 percent, including 54.2 percent of the sheriffs' departments, 88.9 percent of the county police departments, 72.4 percent of the municipal police departments, and 90.0 percent of the state law enforcement agencies sampled.

B.2 DATA ANALYSIS

The data collected by the national survey have been presented so as to provide comparisons across different types of law enforcement agencies, and, for municipal police departments and sheriffs' departments, to compare agencies of different sizes. Because the sample was stratified, comparisons across agency types have been made after weighting the survey responses to reflect the distribution of agency sizes in the universe of agencies.

All analyses have included appropriate tests of statistical significance, although interpretation of those tests has taken account of the fact that they are highly influenced by sample size.

B.3 METHODOLOGICAL CONSTRAINTS

As does all research on the topic of police use of force, this study has limitations. Because this report is based on information derived from a survey providing responses to a self-administered mail survey, completed by representatives selected by the agencies themselves, concerning sensitive topics, the data suffer all the limitations of information produced in that way. Some of the problems generally associated with these aspects of the methodology include: incomplete or inaccurate mailing lists from which samples are drawn, low response rates, differing interpretations of survey items, response bias, and agency unwillingness to provide data on sensitive topics. The Police Foundation used a number of techniques to minimize these constraints, such as obtaining the most complete and current list of law enforcement agencies, writing a concise and clear measurement instrument, using several follow-up techniques to promote response, and so forth. Nonetheless, the limitations of the methodology used can be expected to affect the validity and reliability of the data and should be kept in mind when interpreting the results.

C. THE SURVEY: AN OVERVIEW OF GENERAL FINDINGS

Chapter IV of this report presents the results of the analyses of the survey results by agency type and by agency size, in considerable detail. Below we provide a brief overview of the major findings. First, the report summarizes the overall results across the four agency types— sheriffs' departments, county police departments, city police departments, and state law enforcement agencies. In the subsequent sections, the report highlights important differences across agency types and, within agency types, by agency size.

C.1 USE OF FORCE BY POLICE

The survey conducted by the Police Foundation found that, for most types of force, agencies did not require reports of their use from their officers. The categories of force for which such reporting was most likely to be mandated were those with the most potential for death or serious bodily harm, such as shootings. Similarly, vehicle rammings had to be reported within most departments, and large proportions of all agency types required the reporting of the use of chemical agents, batons, flashlights used as force, and dog attacks. Conversely, small proportions of agencies within all types required the reporting of such categories of force as handcuff use and swarms.

The findings above regarding mandatory reporting have important ramifications for the interpretation of the data provided by departments concerning the use of force by their officers. Because of the lack of mandatory reporting for a number of types of force, a large number of agencies were unable to respond to the survey items requesting information regarding the number of times officers used the various types of force during 1991. Further, several agencies supplied data concerning types of force for which reporting was not mandatory. As a result, those data necessarily came from a voluntary subset of officers.

Recognizing the limitations of the nature of the data, the information provided by departments concerning use of force by their officers was converted to rates per 1,000 sworn officers. According to these estimates, in 1991, the rates at which police used force varied from below one use per 1,000 sworn officers for shootings which resulted in deaths to slightly higher for such types of force as shootings which resulted in injuries, the use of impact devices other than batons or flashlights, the use of neck restraints, and vehicle rammings. Conversely, relatively high rates were reported for the use of bodily force, use of handcuffs, and unholstering of weapons, undoubtedly reflecting the integral part they play in the law enforcement role of police officers.

C.2 FACTORS ASSOCIATED WITH THE USE OF FORCE

Based on the prior literature, the survey elicited information about policies and procedures (such as selection procedures), training, and monitoring, that may affect the rate at which officers use force.

One selection device is to screen out at hiring those officers with a propensity toward unnecessary or excessive force. According to the national survey, an average of at least one-half of agencies, regardless of type, required psychological or psychiatric evaluations of pre-service employees.

Responding agencies provided, on average, between 390 and 790 hours of academy training to recruits, depending on agency type. Between 40 and 95 percent of the agencies within each type followed this training with a formal Field Training Officer (FTO) program. Probationary periods averaged between 8 and 13 months, depending on agency type.

A majority of agencies within each type reported that they reviewed all use of force reports. The remaining departments either reviewed selected reports or reported that they did not review these reports at all.

C.3 CITIZEN COMPLAINTS OF EXCESSIVE FORCE

The survey collected a considerable amount of information concerning citizen complaints of excessive force, including the number of such complaints received, the disposition of those complaints, the characteristics of the complainants and the officers against whom complaints were lodged, and the disposition of those complaints. In addition, information about the process by which complaints are reviewed was collected. This section provides a summary of the information collected concerning those topics.

C.3.1 RATE OF COMPLAINTS RECEIVED

Agencies were requested to provide information concerning the number of complaints of excessive force received in 1991. Approximately three-fourths of the agencies within each type provided such information. In order to provide standardized estimates, an indicator was created representing the number of complaints of excessive force received for every 1,000 sworn personnel. The rates ranged from 15.7 to 47.5 excessive force complaints per 1,000 sworn personnel, depending on agency type and size.

As discussed in Chapter II, the interpretation of citizen complaint rates is not straightfor-ward. High complaint rates, for example, could be indicative of any of a number of various departmental characteristics, including high arrest activity and confidence in the complaint review process among the residents of the jurisdiction. Conversely, low complaint rates could result from low police activity and/or the presence of policies or procedures that discourage citizens from filing complaints. Recognizing these complexities, it is not readily possible to draw conclusions about the extent of police misconduct within individual departments or groups of departments merely on the basis of high or low complaint rates.

C.3.2 DISPOSITIONS OF COMPLAINTS AND DISCIPLINE IMPOSED

Of the 1991 complaints reaching final dispostion in the complaint review process, less than 13 percent within each agency type were sustained. As with the rate of complaints received, findings with regard to complaint dispositions are subject to multiple interpretations. A low sustained rate, for example, could be the result of a number of factors, including, but not limited to, a less than rigorous complaint review process, a high standard of proof for sustaining complaints, or a high rate of false complaints. A high rate of sustained complaints, on the other hand, could represent the absence of all the above-mentioned features.

Of the complaints that were sustained, most resulted in reprimands or suspensions. The severity of discipline meted out is itself subject to multiple interpretations. For example, a large percentage of lower level dispositions (such as reprimands) for sustained complaints may represent the dispensation of punishment appropriately designed for minor misconduct or, on the contrary, may reflect a refusal by the agency to dispense strong sanctions.

C.3.3 CHARACTERISTICS OF COMPLAINANTS AND OFFICERS AGAINST WHOM COMPLAINTS WERE FILED

When, compared to the population, complainants were in general disproportionately black and disproportionately male. Conversely, whites and females were generally underrepresented.

Comparing officers against whom complaints were filed to all officers in the same agencies revealed that male officers were generally overrepresented among those receiving complaints. Neither the race/ethnicity nor the educational levels of officers against whom complaints were filed or sustained differed consistently from that of all officers in their departments across all agencies. (See Chapter 4 for differences within various agency types). Younger and less experienced officers were generally overrepresented among both officers against whom complaints were filed and officers against whom complaints were sustained. It should be considered that younger, less-experienced officers are more likely to be assigned to patrol responsibilities, and therefore to be in more frequent contact with the public.

C.3.4 PROCEDURES FOR PROCESSING COMPLAINTS

As indicated previously, the rate at which departments receive complaints of police misconduct may be a product, in part, of factors related to the solicitation and processing of complaints. Recognizing this fact, the national survey collected information from the sample of departments regarding the processing of complaints, from solicitation to appeals. Flyers, public service announcements, and citizen complaint hotlines were the most popular methods for informing citizens about the complaint filing procedures, though none of these methods was used by more than one-sixth of the agencies within any one agency type. In fact, a majority of the responding departments within each type used none of the six methods listed in the questionnaire for publicizing the complaint process.

With regard to the intake stage of the citizen complaint process, nearly all of the departments, regardless of type, allowed a person to file a complaint in person and a large majority within each type allowed complaints to be filed by mail, over the main department phone, or by telegram.

Virtually all of the responding agencies, regardless of type, had provisions for citizens to file complaints of police misconduct at agency headquarters. The proportion of agencies which allowed complaints to be filed at alternative locations such as city hall, district/precinct stations, or with the Board of Police Commissioners varied, not surprisingly, by agency type.

Approximately half of the city, county, and sheriffs' agencies required that a supervisor accept complaints. By contrast, a majority of state agencies allowed any employee (civilian or sworn) to accept complaints.

Over 70 percent of the agencies within each type allowed citizens to file their complaints at any time during the day. Similarly, a vast majority of the departments had no time limit following the alleged incidents for the filing of complaints of police misconduct.

Forty percent or more of departments within each type provided complaint forms, had officers complete the forms for the citizens, assisted non-English speaking citizens, or informed the citizens of the dispositions of their complaints.

An average of between one-half and three-quarters of agencies, depending upon type, required citizens to sign complaints. The percent of agencies requiring that citizens swear to, notarize, or certify complaints ranged from less than 10 percent among state agencies to 20 percent or higher for other agency types.

Responding agencies also provided information on the survey with regard to the investigation stage of the complaint process. For instance, an average of between 4 and 12 percent of the responding agencies, depending upon type, had a civilian complaint review board or agency. Most of the departments, regardless of type, that did not utilize civilian review assigned the task of reviewing complaints to sworn personnel. Agency types varied considerably in terms of the proportion of agencies which utilized full-time Internal Affairs Units. Of those with such units, most were headed by a person of the rank of lieutenant or above.

Between one-fifth and one-half of the responding departments, depending upon type, indicated that they required complaints be reviewed outside the chain of command of the officer against whom a complaint was filed.

One-half to two-thirds of the agencies indicated that they had no time limit on the investigation process. Between one-quarter and one-third of the agencies within each type required that the investigation be completed within one month.

The right of officers accused of using excessive force to refuse, without penalty, to provide information during investigations of those complaints varied considerably by agency type, from less than 5 percent among state agencies to almost 30 percent among sheriffs' departments.

In two-thirds or more of the departments of all types, the chief executive of the agency had final responsibility for acting on the recommendations for disciplinary action. A vast majority of departments allowed an officer to appeal a decision concerning disciplinary action. Between one-half and three-quarters of the agencies within each type also allowed the citizen to appeal the complaint disposition.

For officers identified as using excessive force, a majority of departments either required counseling or provided it on an optional basis. Within each agency type, one-third or more of the agencies mandated counseling for their identified officers. Similarly, a majority of the departments required retraining or provided it on an optional basis for officers identified as using excessive force. Again, within each agency type, at least one-third of the agencies mandated retraining of these officers.

C.4 CIVIL SUITS AND CRIMINAL CHARGES

To provide a better understanding of the legal and financial consequences of allegations of excessive force, law enforcement agencies were requested to provide information concerning the number of 1991 civil suits and criminal charges alleging use of excessive force, the disposition of those suits and charges, and the amount paid in civil litigation cases in which damages were awarded to the plaintiff. A majority of agencies indicated that they were unable to provide this information because it was not available to them or could not release it publicly. As a result, these findings should be interpreted with caution.

The rate per 1,000 sworn officers of civil suits involving allegations of excessive force ranged from approximately 6 among state agencies to almost 24 for city police departments. Approximately two-thirds of the civil suits were still pending at the time the surveys were returned. Of those with dispositions, most were resolved in or out of court in favor of the defendant (e.g., the officer or department). Even though only a small number of agencies reported suits resolved in favor of the litigant, the total amounts awarded totalled almost $50 million.

Among the agencies providing information, fewer than 1.3 criminal charges per 1,000 sworn officers were reported, regardless of agency type. Of the criminal cases which had been resolved by the time the survey was submitted, slightly less than 60 percent had been resolved in court and most of the resolutions favored the defendant.

D. VARIATIONS ACROSS AGENCY TYPE

As indicated in the methods chapter, comparisons were made between agency types— sheriffs' departments, county police departments, city police departments, and state agencies—based on previous research indicating that their different roles and responsibilities might produce different survey results. This section summarizes, for each agency type, the ways in which they were notably distinguished from the other types.

D.1 SHERIFFS' DEPARTMENTS

D.1.1 REQUIRED REPORTING OF AND USE OF FORCE

Sheriffs' departments were more likely to require the reporting of the use of most types of force than were county police departments and state agencies, but required reporting at approximately the same rate as city police departments.

For most types of force, the rate of use reported by sheriffs' departments was lower than that of city police departments but higher than those of county and state agencies. Sheriffs' departments reported particularly high rates of handcuff use—perhaps reflecting their greater involvement in the service of arrest warrants or their role in supervising jails. Sheriffs' departments also reported high rates of unholsterings of weapons, bodily force, and the use of come-along holds.

D.1.2 FACTORS ASSOCIATED WITH USE OF FORCE

Sheriffs' departments were the least likely of the four types of agencies to require a psychological or psychiatric exam for selection, had the lowest average number of academy training hours, were least likely to have a formal FTO program, and had the shortest average length of probation periods.

D.1.3 CITIZEN COMPLAINTS OF EXCESSIVE FORCE

The rate of complaints per 1,000 officers for sheriffs' departments was lower than the corresponding rate for both city and county agencies, but higher than that for state agencies.

Sheriffs' departments were less likely than the other types of agencies to use multiple methods for informing citizens about the complaint process (e.g., posters, flyers, newsletters), and they were, with city departments, less likely than county police departments and state agencies to allow citizens to file complaints 24 hours a day. Sheriffs' departments were least likely to assist non-English speaking complainants and most likely to require that complainants swear to the complaints.

Of the four types of agencies, sheriffs' departments sustained the lowest percentage of citizen complaints. Sheriffs' departments were also the most likely to handle internal affairs on a case-by-case basis and least likely to have a time limit for the completion of complaint investigations.

Sheriffs' departments were, with city police departments, more likely than county police departments and state agencies to allow accused officers to refuse to cooperate with the investigations. Sheriffs' agencies were also the least likely to provide (optional or mandatory) counseling or retraining to officers identified as using excessive force.

Males and blacks were both overrepresented among persons complaining of excessive force by sheriffs', relative to their presence in the overall population.

Male officers were overrepresented among those against whom complaints of excessive force were filed as well as among those against whom complaints were sustained.

Although officers with college degrees were overrepresented among persons against whom complaints were filed, they were proportionately represented among the officers against whom complaints were sustained.

Younger, less experienced officers were overrepresented among officers against whom complaints were filed and against whom complaints were sustained.

D.2 COUNTY POLICE DEPARTMENTS

D.2.1 REQUIRED REPORTING OF AND USE OF FORCE

County police departments were less likely than sheriffs' departments and city police departments, but more likely than state agencies to mandate the reporting of most types of force.

For most types of force, the rates of use reported by county police departments were higher than those of state agencies, lower than those of city agencies, and comparable to those of sheriffs' departments. The highest rates of force reported by county police departments were for handcuff use and bodily force.

D.2.2 FACTORS ASSOCIATED WITH USE OF FORCE

County police departments did not differ notably from other agency types with regard to their selection procedures, training requirements, and use of force monitoring procedures.

D.2.3 CITIZEN COMPLAINTS OF EXCESSIVE FORCE

County police departments reported the second highest rate of citizen complaints of excessive force per 1,000 sworn personnel of the four agency types. County police departments were the most likely to use posters and flyers to inform citizens of the complaint system. Along with state agencies, county departments were most likely to allow citizens to use each of the various methods for filing complaints—for instance, telegram, or a special phone line; and most likely to allow citizens to file any time of day. Relatively large proportions of county police agencies provided complaint forms to citizens, provided bilingual complaint forms, and had officers complete the forms for the citizens.

More of the county police departments than agencies of the other three types had civilian complaint review boards and were most likely to use Internal Affairs Units for investigations. Of those agencies that had full-time Internal Affairs units, more of the county police departments than any of the other types had heads of those units with the rank of lieutenant or above. County agencies (along with state agencies) were more likely than sheriffs' departments or city police departments to have policies requiring that the review of a complaint occur outside the chain of command of the officer charged.

County police departments sustained a higher percentage of complaints than sheriffs' departments, but a lower percentage than both city police departments and state agencies.

County police departments were less likely than other agency types to give reprimands to officers against whom complaints of excessive force were sustained. On the other hand, county departments were the most likely to suspend such officers.

County police departments were the most likely of all four types to mandate counseling for officers identified as using excessive force and most likely to mandate retraining for these identified officers.

Males and blacks were overrepresented among citizen complainants relative to their proportions in the general population. The complaints of black citizens were less likely to be sustained than were the complaints of white citizens.

Male officers were overrepresented among county police department officers against whom complaints were filed and against whom complaints were sustained. Though blacks were overrepresented among officers against whom complaints were filed, they were underrepresented among officers against whom complaints were sustained. Conversely, white officers were underrepresented among officers against whom complaints were filed and overrepresented among the officers against whom complaints were sustained.

Officers with high school degrees and officers with associates' degrees were overrepresented among county police officers against whom complaints were sustained.

As with other agency types, younger, less experienced officers were overrepresented among county police officers against whom complaints were filed.

D.3 City Police Departments

D.3.1 Required Reporting of and Use of Force

City police departments were more likely than county police departments and state agencies, but about as likely as sheriffs' departments, to mandate the reporting of various types of force.

City departments had the highest rates of use of force in almost half of the force categories. This could be a function of the nature of their role and the environment in which they operate.

D.3.2   FACTORS ASSOCIATED WITH USE OF FORCE

The selection procedures and use of force monitoring procedures of city departments were not notably different from those of other agency types. The academy training of city departments was less extensive than that of state agencies and county police departments, but more extensive than that reported by sheriffs' departments.

D.3.3   CITIZEN COMPLAINTS OF EXCESSIVE FORCE

City agencies had the highest rate of complaints of excessive force. This is consistent with the relatively high levels of force reported by municipal agencies.

Municipal police departments were the most likely to use newsletters for informing citizens of the complaint system, but otherwise were not distinctive in terms of soliciting complaints.

The procedures used to process complaints by city police departments were similar to those used by the other types of agencies, except that city agencies were more likely than the other types to place the final responsibility for disciplining officers with an elected official.

The percent of complaints received by city police departments that were sustained was higher than that reported by sheriffs' departments and county police departments, but lower than that of state agencies. The discipline imposed by city police departments was not notably different from that imposed by the other types of agencies.

Males and blacks were overrepresented among citizens filing complaints against municipal police officers for alleged excessive force. Blacks were less likely, however, to have their complaints sustained.

Male officers were overrepresented among city police officers against whom complaints were filed and against whom complaints were sustained. Whites were underrepresented among officers against whom complaints were filed, but proportionately represented among officers against whom complaints were sustained.

City police officers with high school degrees or with associates' degrees were overrepresented among officers against whom complaints were sustained.

D.4   STATE AGENCIES

D.4.1   REQUIRED REPORTING OF AND USE OF FORCE

State agencies were the least likely of all four types to mandate the reporting of the use of force by their officers. State agencies also reported the lowest rates of the use of force in a majority of categories.

D.4.2 FACTORS ASSOCIATED WITH USE OF FORCE

State agencies were the most likely to require a psychological or psychiatric exam of potential recruits and had the highest average number of academy training hours. They were more likely than the other types of agencies to have a formal FTO program and had the longest probationary periods for new officers. State agencies were the least likely, however, to review all force reports.

D.4.3 CITIZEN COMPLAINTS OF EXCESSIVE FORCE

State agencies had the lowest rates of complaints of excessive force.

State agencies were generally the least likely to use the various methods listed in the survey (such as flyers and posters) for informing citizens about the complaint process. State agencies were also the least likely to have a restriction on the amount of time after the alleged event during which citizens could file complaints, but least likely to provide complainants with copies of the complaints. They were most likely to allow any employee (e.g., not just sworn supervisors or sworn personnel) to accept complaints and least likely to require that citizens swear to the complaints.

State agencies were the least likely to report that they had civilian review boards. A greater proportion of state agencies than any of the other types had time limits for the investigation of complaints.

While they reported the lowest rate of complaints, state agencies reported the highest rate of sustained complaints of the four types of agencies. State agencies were the least likely to allow a citizen to appeal the disposition of the complaint.

State agencies were the most likely to impose a reprimand following a sustained complaint and the least likely to suspend officers.

State agencies were the most likely to provide mandatory or optional counseling or retraining to officers identified as using excessive force.

Males were overrepresented among persons filing complaints of excessive force against state officers. Unlike the pattern found among other agency types, however, whites and persons of "other" race/ethnicity, rather than blacks, were overrepresented among complainants. Blacks and Hispanics, however, were overrepresented among persons whose complaints against state officers were sustained.

In contrast to the pattern found among the other agency types, males were not overrepresented among state officers against whom complaints were filed or against whom complaints were sustained. Black officers, however, were overrepresented among officers against whom complaints were filed and against whom complaints were sustained.

Officers with associate's degrees were overrepresented among officers against whom complaints were filed, but those with high school degrees were overrepresented among officers against whom complaints were sustained.

In contrast to the other agency types, older state officers were overrepresented among officers against whom complaints were filed and among officers against whom complaints were sustained. However, consistent with the other agencies, officers against whom complaints were filed and against whom complaints were sustained had less experience than the average officer.

E. VARIATIONS ACROSS AGENCY SIZE

Among sheriffs' and city police departments, comparisons were made among agencies of various sizes. (Due to the small numbers of county police departments and state agencies, such comparisons were not appropriate among those types.) This section summarizes the major findings of those comparisons, focusing especially on those that were consistent for both sheriffs' departments and city agencies.

E.1 REQUIRED REPORTING OF AND USE OF FORCE

Generally, larger city and sheriffs' departments were most likely to mandate that certain types of force used by their officers be reported. The exception for both types of agencies was for unholstering weapons.

Consistent with the literature on deadly force, larger departments reported higher rates at which citizens were shot at and either wounded or killed. The rates at which other types of force were used did not vary consistently between large and small departments.

E.2 FACTORS ASSOCIATED WITH USE OF FORCE

Among both city police and sheriffs' departments, larger agencies were more likely to require psychological or psychiatric exams during their officer selection process. Large agencies also had, on average, longer academy training periods and were more likely to have formal FTO programs for trainees following academy training.

E.3 CITIZEN COMPLAINTS OF EXCESSIVE FORCE

Although larger city police departments had more complaints per 1,000 sworn officers than smaller departments, this relationship was not replicated among sheriffs' departments.

The larger sheriffs' and city police departments were more likely to use multiple methods to solicit citizen complaints as well as more likely to allow complaints to be filed by mail, telegram, or over a separate telephone line. Large departments were also more likely to accept complaints at district/precinct stations, storefront or mini-stations, or at civilian review board offices, and more likely to allow any employee to accept complaints. Large departments were more likely than small departments to allow for the filing of complaints at any time of day and, generally, provided more assistance to persons lodging complaints. One exception was that smaller departments were more likely to inform the complainants of any disciplinary action taken against the officers about whom they had complained.

Although more of the larger city departments than smaller city departments had civilian review boards, this relationship was not found among sheriffs' departments. Greater proportions of the larger municipal and sheriffs' departments had specialized units (such as Internal Affairs Units or Offices of Professional Standards) to investigate complaints. The larger the department, the higher the rank of the person in charge of the Internal Affairs Unit. Larger departments were also more likely to require that a complaint review occur outside the chain of command of the accused officer. A smaller proportion of larger, compared to smaller, agencies allowed officers against whom complaints were filed to refuse, without penalty, to provide information during investigations of those complaints.

Larger departments were more likely to place time limits on the investigation of complaints, less likely to allow citizens to file appeals of dispositions, and more likely to publish summary information regarding complaints.

Among city departments, smaller agencies were more likely to sustain complaints of excessive force than were larger ones. This pattern was not found among sheriffs' departments. No differences were apparent with regard to the discipline imposed by large and small departments.

F.   DISCUSSION AND IMPLICATIONS

This report has presented the findings of a national survey of law enforcement agencies documenting the extent to which their officers use various types of force, how those agencies attempt to monitor and control the use of such force, the number and disposition of citizen complaints of excessive force, and the number and disposition of civil suits and criminal charges alleging excessive force. In addition, the survey obtained information concerning a large number of factors that, based on existing literature, may be associated with the use of force, citizen complaints, and related issues.

Given the controversial nature of the topics addressed, the response to the survey was gratifyingly high. A great deal of information has been generated, much of it for the first time, that sheds light on a wide range of facets of the use of force among police officers, department policies and procedures designed to regulate the use of force, and the ways in which departments deal with allegations of excessive force.

Much work remains to be done to take full advantage of the information and insights produced by this work. From the perspective of practitioners, this research has made it clear that more systematic and standardized methods of defining and reporting the use of various types of force are called for. A sharing of information about what methods are currently used to monitor and control the use of force is also in order.

From the research standpoint, the massive amount of data collected during the course of this study are ripe for further analysis. More sophisticated analyses of the reported use of force should be conducted that control for such activity measures as calls for service and arrest rates. Multivariate analyses of the relationships between the rates of reported use of various types of force and the multitude of factors hypothesized to be related to such use need to be conducted. Similar analyses should be performed examining the reported rates of citizen complaints of excessive force and the many factors thought to affect those rates. Further, an empirical analysis of the effects, if any, of different methods of handling citizen complaints on the disposition of those complaints would be valuable.

Such analyses, and many more, should be the next step in a continuing exploration of the issue of police use of force. In addition, to fully understand the meaning and significance of the data produced by the national survey of law enforcement agencies, it is necessary to conduct intensive case studies to determine exactly how and why the enormous differences—in reported use of force, citizen complaints, and disposition of those complaints—noted in this study occur. The lessons learned from those analyses must be presented in clear fashion and widely disseminated among both practitioners and scholars.

Finally, one of the most important lessons of this study is the finding that so little is known about such a critical topic—the extent, nature, causes, and methods of dealing with police use of force. Data such as those collected by this study should be collected and analyzed on a periodic basis, providing a barometer of the national state of use of force by our police officers. Before such an effort can be fully effective, however, more agencies should be encouraged to require the reporting by their officers of their use of various types of force.

The research presented in this report resembles in many respects the work that led to the creation of the Uniform Crime Reports (UCR) system. During the late 1890's and the first two decades of this century, police chiefs and others argued the necessity of some national clearinghouse for crime statistics. As recounted by Walker (1977), the International Association of Chiefs of Police began a rudimentary collection of criminal records in 1897. In the 1920's, several states began maintaining their own crime statistics. By 1928, preliminary work began on creating a federal crime records system. The final creation of the UCR system in 1930, however, did not occur until a heightened sense of national concern about crime arose, a concern which was prompted largely by a few spectacular and well-publicized incidents, such as gangland killings in Chicago. For the first several years of its existence, the UCR system strived to gain compliance from local police departments and sought to overcome innumerable flaws in the reporting methods.

After almost sixty years, the Uniform Crime Reports system has become widely accepted and respected. Ironically, law enforcement agencies are often held accountable for variations in the rates of crime reported by that system, despite the fact that those agencies are by no means solely responsible for the phenomenon of crime.

Just as with the Uniform Crime Reports system, the creation of such a system will require the concentrated effort of many committed individuals and organizations—over a long period of time. Resistance is to be expected. Refinements will be necessary. Even more than the UCR, however, the systematic collection of data on the use of force by police would provide information about activities that are, to a much greater degree than crime, under the control of the police themselves.

In the same way that the Uniform Crime Reports system was created as a useful response to several celebrated instances of crime during the 1920's, so the creation of a system to collect data on police use of force would be a constructive response to the celebrated incidents of such force in the last few years.

REFERENCES

Alpert, Geoffrey P. and Lorie A. Fridell (1992). *Police Vehicles and Firearms: Instruments of Deadly Force.* Prospect Heights, IL: Waveland Press.

American Civil Liberties Union (1991). *On the Line: Police Brutality and its Remedies.* New York, NY: ACLU.

Barker, Thomas (1978). An empirical study of police deviance other than corruption. *Journal of Police Science and Administration* 6(3): 264-272. Reprinted in Thomas Barker, and David L. Carter, Eds. (1991). *Police Deviance*, Second Edition, pp. 123-138. Cincinnati, OH: Anderson.

Babbie, Earl (1990). *Survey Research Methods*, Second Edition. Belmont, California: Wadsworth Publishing Company.

Barker, Thomas and David L. Carter (1991). A typology of police deviance. In Barker, Thomas and David L. Carter, Eds. *Police Deviance*, Second Edition, pp. 3-12. Cincinnati, OH: Anderson.

Barton, Peter G. (1970). Civilian review boards and the handling of complaints against the police. *University of Toronto Law Journal* 20:448-469.

Bayley, David H. and Harold Mendelsohn (1969). *Minorities and the Police: Confrontation in America.* New York: Free Press.

Bayley, David H. and James Garofalo (1987). *Patrol Officer Effectiveness in Managing Conflict During Police-Citizen Encounters.* Report to the New York State Commission on Criminal Justice and the Use of Force. Volume III.

_____ (1989). The management of violence by police patrol officers. *Criminology* 27(1):1-25.

Berel, Harold and Marcus Sisk (1964). The administration of complaints by citizens against police. *Harvard Law Review* LXXVII: 499-519.

Binder, Arnold and Peter Scharf (1980). The violent police-citizen encounter. *_Annals of the American Academy of Political and Social Science* 452: 111-121.

Binder, Arnold; Peter Scharf and Raymond Galvin (1982). *Use of Deadly Force by Police Officers.* Final report submitted to the National Institute of Justice, Grant No. 79-NI-AX-0134.

Bittner, Egon (1967). The police on skid row: A study of peacekeeping. *_American Sociological Review* 32(5):699-715.

_____ (1970). *The Functions of Police in Modern Society.* Washington, DC: U.S. Government Printing Office.

Black, Algernon D. (1968). *The People and the Police.* New York: McGraw Hill.

Black, Donald J. and Albert J. Reiss Jr. (1967). Patterns of behavior in police and citizen transactions. *Field Surveys III, Studies in Crime and Law Enforcement in Major Metropolitan Areas,* Volume 2. Washington, DC: Government Printing Office.

Black, D. and A.J. Reiss, Jr. (1970). Police control of juveniles. *American Sociological Review* 35(February): 63-77.

Blumberg, Mark (1981). Race and police shootings: Analysis in two cities. In Fyfe, James J., Ed. *Contemporary Issues in Law Enforcement,* 152-166. Beverly Hills, CA: Sage.

_____ (1983). *The Use of Firearms by Police Officers: The Impact of Individuals, Communities and Race.* Ph.D. Dissertation, State University of New York at Albany.

Box, Steven and Ken Russell (1975). The politics of discreditability: Disarming complaints against the police. *Sociological Review* 23(2):315-346.

Bray, Robert J. (1962). Philadelphia's police advisory board: A new concept in community relations. *Villanova Law Review* 8(Summer): 656-673.

Broadaway, Fred M. (1974). Police misconduct: Positive alternatives. *Journal of Police Science and Administration* 2(2):210-218.

Brodsky, Stanley L. and Glenda D. Williamson (1985). Attitudes of police toward violence. *Psychological Reports* 57(3): 1179-80.

Brown, David C. (1983). *Civilian Review of Complaints Against the Police: A Survey of the United States Literature.* London, England: Home Office Research and Planning Unit. Unpublished report.

Campbell, Angus and Howard Schuman (1969). Racial attitudes in fifteen American cities. *Supplemental Studies for the National Advisory Commission on Civil Disorders.* Washington, DC: U.S. Government Printing Office.

Carter, David L. (1984). Theoretical dimensions in the abuse of authority by police officers. *Police Studies* 7(4):224-236.

Cascio, W.F. (1977). Formal education and police officer performance. *Journal of Police Science and Administration* 5(1):89-96.

Chevigny, Paul (1969). *Police Power: Police Abuses in New York City*. New York: Pantheon Books.

Clede, Bill (1987). *Police Nonlethal Force Manual*. Harrisburg, PA: Stackpole Books.

Cohen, B. and J.M. Chaiken (1972). *Police Background Characteristics and Performance: Summary*. New York: Rand Institute.

Coxe, Spencer (1961). Police advisory board: The Philadelphia story. *The*

Connecticut Bar Journal 35:138-155.

____ (1965). The Philadelphia Police Advisory Board. *Law in Transition Quarterly* 2:179-185.

Croft, E.B. (1985). *Police Use of Force: An Empirical Analysis*. Ph.D.

Dissertation, State University of New York at Albany.

____ (1987). *Police Use of Force in Rochester and Syracuse, New York: 1984 and 1985*. Report to the New York State Commission on Criminal Justice and the Use of Force. Volume III.

Culver, John H. (1975). Policing the police: Problems and perspectives. *Journal of Police Science and Administration* 3(2):125-135.

Decker, Scott H. and Allen E. Wagner (1982). Race and citizen complaints against the police: An analysis of their interaction. In Jack Green, Ed. *The Police and the Public*. Beverly Hills: Sage.

Dempsey, R.R. (1972). Police disciplinary systems. *Police Chief* 39(5): 52-6.

Desmedt, John C. (1984). Use of force paradigm for law enforcement. *Journal of Police Science and Administration*. 12(2): 170-176.

Dillman, Don A. (1972). Increasing mail questionnaire response in large samples of the general public. *Public Opinion Quarterly* 36: 254-257.

____ (1978). *Mail and Telephone Surveys: The Total Design Method*. New York: John Wiley & Sons.

____ (1983). Mail and other self-administered questionnaires. In Peter H. Rossi, James D. Wright, and Andy B. Anderson, Eds. *Handbook of Survey Research*, pp. 359-377. New York: Academic Press.

Dillman, D.A.; J.A. Christenson; E.H. Carpenter and R.M. Brooks (1974). Increasing mail questionnaire response: A four state comparison. *American Sociological Review* 39: 744-756.

Doerner, William (1991). Police unholstering and shooting behavior under

simulated field conditions. *American Journal of Police* 10(3):1-15.

Dugan, John R. and Daniel R. Breda (1991). Complaints about police officers: A comparison among types and agencies. *Journal of Criminal Justice* 19(2): 165-171.

Federal Bureau of Investigation (1991). *Use of Unauthorized Force by Law*

Enforcement Personnel: Problems and Solutions. Washington, DC: U.S. Department of Justice.

Fridell, Lorie (1983). *Community Attitudes Toward Police Use of Deadly Force*. Unpublished Master's Thesis, University of California, Irvine.

____ (1989). Justifiable use of measures in research on deadly force. *Journal of Criminal Justice* 17: 157-165

Fridell, Lorie and Arnold Binder (1989). Racial aspects of police shootings revisited. Paper presented at the annual meeting of the American Society of Criminology, Reno, Nevada.

Fridell, Lorie and Arnold Binder (1992). Police officer decision-making in potentially violent confrontations. *Journal of Criminal Justice* 20:385-399.

Friedrich, Robert J. (1977). *The Impact of Organizational, Individual, and*

Situational Factors on Police Behavior. Ph.D. Dissertation, University of Michigan.

____ (1980). Police use of force: Individuals, situations, and organizations. *Annals of the American Academy of Political and Social Science* 452(November): 82-97.

Fuller, Lou L. (1964). *The Morality of Law*. New Haven, CT: Yale University Press.

Fyfe, James J. (1978). *Shots Fired: Examination of New York City Police Firearms Discharges*. Unpublished Dissertation, State University of New York, Albany.

____ (1979). Administrative interventions on police shooting discretion. *Journal of Criminal Justice* 7(4):309-324.

____ (1980a). Always prepared: Police off-duty guns. *Annals of the American Academy of Political and Social Science* 452: 72-81.

____ (1980b). Geographic correlates of police shooting: A microanalysis. *Journal of Research in Crime and Delinquency* 17: 101-113.

___ (1981a). Who shoots? A look at officer race and police shooting. *Journal of Police Science and Administration* 9: 367-382.

___ (1981b). Race and extreme police-citizen violence. In R.L. McNeely and Carl E. Pope, Eds. *Race, Crime and Criminal Justice*, pp. 89-108. Beverly Hills, CA: Sage Publishers.

___ (1981c). Toward a typology of police shootings. In James J. Fyfe, Ed. *Contemporary Issues in Law Enforcement.* pp. 136-151. Beverly Hills, CA: Sage.

___ (1982). Blind justice: Police shootings in Memphis. *Journal of Criminal Law and Criminology* 83: 707-722.

___ (1987a). *The Metro-Dade Police/Citizen Violence Reduction Project.* An unpublished report submitted to the Metro-Dade Police Department by the Police Foundation.

Geller, William A. and Kevin J. Karales (1981). *Split-Second Decisions: Shootings of and by Chicago Police.* Chicago, IL: Chicago Law Enforcement Study Group.

___ (1982). Deadly force: What we know. *Journal of Police Science and Administration* 10: 151-177.

Geller, William A. and Michael Scott (1991). *Deadly Force: What we Know—A Practitioner's Desk Reference on Police - Involved Shootings in the United States.* Washington, DC: Police Executive Research Forum.

Gellhorn, Walter (1966). Police review boards: Hoax or hope? *Columbia University Forum,* Summer: 5-10.

Goldsmith, Andrew and Stuart Farson (1987). Complaints against the police in Canada: A new approach. *The Criminal Law Review* pp. 616-623.

Goldsmith, A.J. (1988). New directions in police complaint procedures: Some conceptual and comparative departures. *Police Studies* 11:60-71.

Groves, W.E. and P.H. Rossi (1970). Police perceptions of a hostile ghetto. *American Behavioral Scientist* 13:727-744.

Hadar, Ilana and John R. Snortum (1975). The eye of the beholder: Differential perceptions of police by the police and the public. *Criminal Justice and Behavior* 2: 284-315.

Hage, Jerald (1980). *Theories of Organization.* New York: Academic Press.

Hansen, Morris H.; William N. Hurwitz and William G. Madow (1953). *Sample Survey Methods and Theory,* Volume I. New York: John Wiley & Sons, Inc.

Harding, Richard W. and Richard P. Fahey (1973). Killings by Chicago police, 1966-1970: An empirical study. *Southern California Law Review* 46: 284-315.

Hartjen, Clayton A. (1972). Police-citizen encounters: Social order in interpersonal interaction. *Criminology* 10(May): 61-84.

Hensley, Terry (1988). Civilian review boards: A means to police accountability. *The Police Chief,* September: 45-47.

Hiatt, D. and G.E. Hargrave (1988). Predicting job performance problems with psychological screening. *Journal of Police Science and Administration* 16:122-125.

Hoffman, Paul (n.d.). The feds, lies, and videotape: *The need for an effective federal role in controlling police abuse in urban America.* Unpublished document. Los Angeles: ACLU Foundation of Southern California.

Hudson, James R. (1970). Police-citizen encounters that lead to citizen complaints. *Social Problems* 18(2): 179-193.

___ (1971). Police review boards and police accountability. *Law and Contemporary Problems* 36:515-538.

___ (1972). Organizational aspects of internal and external review of the police.

Journal of Criminal Law, Criminology and Police Science 63(3):427-433.

Iannone, N.F. (1987). *Supervision of Police Personnel,* Fourth Edition. Englewood Cliffs, NJ: Prentice-Hall, Inc.

Independent Commission on the Los Angeles Police Department (1991). *Report of the Independent Commission of the Los Angeles Police Department.*

International Association of Chiefs of Police (1976). *Managing for Effective Police Discipline.* Gaithersburg, MD: IACP.

Jolin, Annette I. and Don C. Gibbons (1984). Policing the police: The Portland experience. *Journal of Police Science and Administration* 12(3):315-322.

Jones, B., S. Greenberg, C. Kaufman and J. Drew (1977). Bureaucratic response to citizen initiated contacts: Environmental enforcement in Detroit. *American Political Science Review* 72:148-165.

Jones, B. (1980). *Service Delivery in the City*. New York: Longman.

Kahn, R. (1975). Urban reform and police accountability in New York City:

1950-1974. In R. Lineberry Ed., *Urban Problems and Public Policy*. Lexington, MA: Lexington Books.

Kania, Richard R.E. and Wade C. Mackey (1977). Police violence as a function of community characteristics. *Criminology* 15(1):27-48.

Kerstetter, Wayne A. (1985). Who disciplines the police? Who should? In Geller, William A. (Ed.) *Police Leadership in America: Crisis and Opportunity*, pp. 149-182. New York, NY: Praeger.

Kerstetter, Wayne A. and Barrik Van Winkle (1989). *Evidence in investigations of police use of excessive force in Chicago*. Unpublished manuscript.

Klockars, Carl (1980). The Dirty Harry problem. *Annals of the American Academy of Political and Social Science* 452(November): 33-47.

___ (1985). *The Idea of Police*. Beverly Hills, CA: Sage.

Kolts, James G. & Staff (1992). *The Los Angeles Sheriff's Department*. A published report presented to the Board of Supervisors of Los Angeles County, Los Angeles, CA.

Langworthy, Robert H. (1986). Police shooting and criminal homicide: The temporal relationship. *Journal of Quantitative Criminology* 2: 377-388.

Law Enforcement Assistance Administration (1980). *Prevention and Control of Urban Disorders: Issues for the 1980s*. Washington, DC: University Research Corporation.

Letman, Sloan T. (1981). The Office of Professional Standards. *The Police Chief*, March: 44-46.

Littlejohn, Edward J. (1981). The civilian police commission: A deterrent of police misconduct. *Journal of Urban Law* 59(5):5-62.

Lundman, R.; R.E. Sykes, and J.P. Clark (1978). Police control of juveniles. *Journal of Research in Crime and Delinquency* 15(1):74-91.

Lundstrom, Ross and Cynthia Mullan (1987). The use of force: One department's experience. *FBI Law Enforcement Bulletin*, January: 6-9.

McLaughlin, Vance (1992). *Use of force by law enforcement officers: Problems in doing research*. Paper presented at the annual meeting of the Academy of Criminal Justice Sciences in Pittsburgh, Pennsylvania, March 13.

Manning, Peter K. (1980). Violence and the police role. *Annals of the American Academy of Political and Social Science* 452(November): 135-144.

Maquire, M. (1991). Complaints against the police: The British experience. In A. Goldsmith Ed. *Complaints Against the Police: The Trend to External Review*. Oxford, England: Clarendon Press.

Matulia, Kenneth (1982). *A Balance of Forces*. Gaithersburg, MD: International Association of Chiefs of Police.

Matulia, Kenneth (1985). *A Balance of Forces*, Second Edition. Gaithersburg, MD: International Association of Chiefs of Police.

Meyer, Marshall W. (1980). Police shootings at minorities: The case of Los Angeles. *Annals of the American Academy of Political and Social Sciences* 452: 98-110.

Milton, Catherine H.; Jeanne W. Halleck; James Lardner; and Gary L. Abrecht (1977). *Police Use of Deadly Force*. Washington, DC: The Police Foundation.

Morrison, Denton E. and Henkel, Ramon E. (1970). *The Significance Tests Controversy—A Reader*. Chicago: Aldine Publishing Co.

Muir, William Ker, Jr. (1980). Power attracts violence. *Annals of the American Academy of Political and Social Sciences* 452 (November): 48-52.

National Advisory Commission on Criminal Justice Standards and Goals, Task Force on Police (1973). *Police*. Washington, DC: Government Printing Office.

Nevin, H.R. and N.M. Ford (1976). Effects of a deadline and a veiled threat on mail survey responses. *Journal of Applied Psychology* 61:116-118.

New York City Police Department Civilian Complaint Review Board (1986). *Nationwide Survey of Civilian Complaint Systems*. New York: NY: New York City Police Department Civilian Complaint Review Board.

New York City, Civilian Complaint Investigative Bureau (1990). *Annual Report*. New York: Civilian Complaint Investigative Bureau.

New York State Commission on Criminal Justice and the Use of Force (1987). Report to the Governor, Volumes I to IV. New York: New York State.

Pate, Antony M. and Edwin E. Hamilton (1991). *The Big Six: Policing America's Largest Cities*. Washington, DC: The Police Foundation.

Perez, Douglas (1978). *Police accountability: A question of balance.* Ph.D. Dissertation, University of California, Berkeley.

Petersen, D.M. (1972). Police disposition of the petty offender. *Sociology and Social Research* 56(3):320-330.

Peterson, Werner E. (1991). Police accountability and civilian oversight of policing: An American Perspective. In Andrew J. Goldsmith Ed., *Complaints Against the Police: The Trend to External Review.* Oxford: Clarendon Press.

Piliavin, Irving and Scott Briar (1964). Police encounters with juveniles. *American Journal of Sociology* 70(September): 206-214.

President's Commission on Civil Rights (1947). *To Secure These Rights.* New York: Simon and Schuster.

____ (1961). *The 50 States Report.* Washington, DC: U.S. Government Printing Office.

President's Commission on Law Enforcement and Administration of Justice (1967). *Task Force Report: The Police.* Washington, DC: U.S. Government Printing Office.

Reaves, Brian A. (1992A). *Law Enforcement Management and Administrative Statistics, 1990: State and Local Police Departments, 1990.* Bureau of Justice Statistics Bulletin. Washington, DC: U.S. Department of Justice.

Reaves, Brian A. (1992B). *Law Enforcement Management and Administrative Statistics, 1990: Sheriffs' Departments, 1990.* Bureau of Justice Statistics Bulletin. Washington, DC: U.S. Department of Justice.

Reaves, Brian A. (1992C). *Law Enforcement Management and Administrative Statistics, 1990: Data for Individual State and Local Agencies with 100 or More Officers.* Washington, DC: U.S. Department of Justice.

Reaves, Brian A. (1993). City and County Police Departments Data. Correspondence dated September 30. Bureau of Justice Statistics. Washington, DC: U.S. Department of Justice.

Reiss, Albert J. Jr. (1968). Police brutality: Answers to key questions. *Transaction* 5(1968): 10-19.

____ (1971). *The Police and the Public.* New Haven: Yale University Press.

____ (1980). Controlling police use of deadly force. *Annals of the American Academy of Political and Social Science* 452: 122-134.

Robin, Gerald D. (1963). Justifiable homicide by police officers. *Journal of Criminal Law, Criminology and Police Science* 54: 225-231.

Schwartz, Louis B. (1970). Complaints against the police: Experience of the community rights division of the Philadelphia district attorney's office. *University of Pennsylvania Law Review* 118: 1023-1035.

Scharf, Peter and Arnold Binder (1983). *The Badge and the Bullet: Police Use of Deadly Force.* New York, NY: Praeger.

Sharp, Elaine B. (1984). Need, awareness, and contacting propensity: Study of a city with a central complaint unit. *Urban Affairs Quarterly* 20(1): 22-30.

Sherman, Lawrence W. and Robert Langworthy (1979). Measuring homicide by police officers. *Journal of Criminal Law and Criminology* 70: 546-560.

Sherman, Lawrence W. (1980). Causes of police behavior: The current state of quantitative research. *Journal of Research in Crime and Delinquency* 17(1): 69-100.

____ (1983). Reducing police gun use: Critical events, administrative policy and organizational change. In Maurice Punch, Ed. *The Management and Control of Police Organizations,* pp. 98-125. Cambridge, MA: M.I.T. Press.

Sherman, Lawrence W.; Ellen G. Cohn; Patrick R. Gartin; Edwin E. Hamilton; and Dennis P. Rogan (1986). *Citizens Killed by Big City Police, 1970-1984.* Washington, DC: Crime Control Institute.

Skolnick, J.H. (1966). *Justice Without Trial: Law Enforcement in a Democratic Society.* New York, NY: John Wiley & Sons, Inc.

Skolnick, Jerome H. and James J. Fyfe (1993). *Above the Law: Police and the Excessive Use of Force.* New York: The Free Press.

Slovak, Jeffrey S. (1986). *Styles of Urban Policing: Organization, Environment, and Police Styles in Selected American Cities.* New York: New York University Press.

Smith, Douglas (1986). The neighborhood context of police behavior. In Reiss, Albert J., Jr. and Michael Tonry, Eds. *Communities and Crime,* pp. 313-341. Chicago, IL: University of Chicago Press.

____ (1987). Police response to interpersonal violence: Defining the parameters of legal control. *Social Forces* 65(3): 767-782.

Smith, Joseph L. (1974). Police inspection and complaint reception procedures. *FBI Law Enforcement Bulletin*, February: 12-15.

Smith, Paul E. and Richard O. Hawkins (1973). Victimization, types of citizen- police contacts, and attitudes toward the police. *Law and Society Review* 8:135-152.

Spradley, James P. (1970). *You Owe Yourself a Drunk: An Ethnography of Urban Nomads*. Boston: Little, Brown.

St. Clair, James D. (1992). *Report of the Boston Police Department Management Review Committee*. Unpublished report submitted to Mayor Raymond Flynn, Boston, Massachusetts.

Stoddard, Ellwyn R. (1968). The "informal code" of police deviancy: A group approach to "blue coat" crime. *Journal of Criminal Law, Criminology, and Police Science* 59(2): 201-213.

Sykes, R. and J.P. Clark (1975). A theory of deference exchange in police-civilian encounters. *American Journal of Sociology* 81(3): 584-600.

Sykes, Richard E. and Edward E. Brent (1980). The regulation of interaction by police: A systems view of taking charge. *Criminology* 18(2):182-197.

___ (1983). *Policing: A Social Behaviorist Perspective*. New Brunswick, New Jersey: Rutgers University Press.

Task Force on the Police (1967). *Task Force Report: The Police*. Washington, DC: The President's Commission on Law Enforcement and the Administration of Justice.

Ten-Brink, William and David Lester (1984). Reporting fellow police officers for brutality: A preliminary study. *Psychological Reports* 54(1): 36.

Terrill, Richard J. (1982). Complaint procedures: Variations on the theme of civilian participation. *Journal of Police Science and Administration* 10(4): 398-407.

___ (1990). Alternative perceptions of independence in civilian oversight. *Journal of Police Science and Administration* 17(2): 77-83.

Terry, Don (1992). Kansas City police go after their "bad boys." *New York Times*, September 10, p. A1.

Toch, Hans (1969). *Violent Men: An Inquiry into the Psychology of Violence*. Chicago, IL: Aldine. [Revised edition, 1984, Cambridge, MA: Schenkman.]

Toch, Hans; J. Douglas Grant, and Raymond T. Galvin (1975). *Agents of Change: A Study in Police Reform*. New York, NY: John Wiley & Sons.

Toch, Hans (1976). *Peacekeeping: Police, Prisons and Violence*. Lexington, MA: D.C. Heath.

___ (1980). Mobilizing police expertise. *Annals of the American Academy of Political and Social Science*. 452 (November): 53-62.

___ (1985). The catalytic situation in the violence equation. *Journal of Applied Social Psychology* 15(2): 105-123.

Topping, Ivan (1987). The police complaints system in Northern Ireland. *Police Journal* 60(3): 252-263.

Uchida, Craig Dennis (1982). *Controlling Police Use of Deadly Force: Organizational Change in Los Angeles*. Unpublished Dissertation, State University of New York, Albany.

Uelman, Gerald F. (1973). Varieties of public policy: A study of policy regarding the use of deadly force in Los Angeles County. *University of Loyola at Los Angeles Law Review* 6: 1-65.

United States Commission on Civil Rights (1978). *Police Practices and the Preservation of Civil Rights*. Washington, DC: Government Printing Office.

___ (1981). *Who is Guarding the Guardians? A Report on Police Practices*. Washington, DC: Government Printing Office.

U.S. Department of Justice, Civil Rights Division, Criminal Section (1991). *Police Brutality Study*. Washington, DC: U.S. Department of Justice.

Van Maan, John (1974). Working the street: A developmental view of police behavior. in Herbert Jacob, Ed. *The Potential for Reform of Criminal Justice*, pp. 83-130. Beverly Hills: Sage.

Waegel, William B. (1984). The use of lethal force by police: The effect of statutory change. *Crime and Delinquency* 31: 121-140.

Wagner, A.E. (1980a). Citizen complaints against the police: The complainant. *Journal of Police Science and Administration* 8: 247-252.

___ (1980b). Citizen complaints against the police: The accused officer. *Journal of Police Science and Administration* 8: 373-377.

Wagner, Allen E. and Scott H. Decker (1993). Evaluating citizen complaints against the police. In

Roger G. Dunham and Geoffrey P. Alpert, Eds. *Critical Issues in Policing: Contemporary Readings*, second edition, pp. 275-291. Prospect Heights, IL: Waveland Press, Inc.

Walker, Roy O. (1982). Exploratory investigation of police attitudes toward violence. *Journal of Police Science and Administration* 10(1): 93-100.

Walker, Samuel (1977). *A Critical History of Police Reform: The Emergence of Professionalism*. Lexington, Massachusetts: Lexington Books.

____ (1980). *Popular Justice: A History of American Criminal Justice*. New York: Oxford University Press.

Walker, Samuel and Vic W. Bumphus (1992). The effectiveness of civilian review: Observations on recent trends and new issues regarding the civilian review of the police. *American Journal of Police* XI(4): 1-26.

Walker, Samuel and Lorie Fridell (1993). Forces of change in police policy: The impact of *Tennessee v. Garner* on deadly force policy. *American Journal of Police* 11(3): 97-112.

Walker, Samuel and Vic W. Bumphus (1992). The effectiveness of civilian review: Observations on recent trends and new issues regarding the civilian review of police. *American Journal of Police* XI(4): 1-26.

Warwick, Donald P. and Charles A. Lininger (1975). *The Sample Survey: Theory and Practice*. New York: McGraw-Hill Book Company.

Watt, Susan (1991). The future of civilian oversight of policing. *Canadian Journal of Criminology*, July-October: 347-362.

Weisheit, Ralph A., Falcone, David N. and Wells, L. Edward (1993). *Rural Crime and Rural Policing: An Overview of the Issues*. Normal, IL: Illinois State University, Draft - Version 9.2.

Weiss, Alexander (1992). *The Innovation Process in Public Organizations: Patterns of Diffusion and Adoption in American Policing*. Ph.D. Dissertation, Northwestern University.

Weitzer, Ronald (1986). Accountability and complaints against the police in Northern Ireland. *Police Studies* 9(2): 99-109.

West, Paul (1988). Investigation of complaints against the police: Summary report of a national survey. *American Journal of Police* 7(2): 101-121.

____ (1991). Investigation and review of complaints against police officers: An overview of issues and philosophies. In Thomas Barker and David L. Carter, Eds. *Police Deviance*, second edition, pp. 373-399. Cincinnati, Ohio: Anderson Publishing.

Westley, W.A. (1953). Violence and the police. *American Journal of Sociology* 59(July): 34-41.

____ (1970). *Violence and the Police: A Sociological Study of Law, Custom, and Morality*. Cambridge, MA: The MIT Press.

Whitaker, G. (1982). *Basic Issues in Policing*. Washington, DC: U.S. Government Printing Office.

Wickersham Commission (1931). *Report on Lawlessness in Law Enforcement*. National Commission on Law Observance and Enforcement. Washington, DC: U.S. Government Printing Office.

Wiley, M.G. and T.L. Hudik (1974). Police-citizen encounters: A field test of exchange theory. *Social Problems* 22(October): 119-127.

Williams, J.S.; C.W. Thomas; and B.K. Singh (1983). Situational use of police force: Public reactions. *American Journal of Police* 3(1): 37-50.

Wilson, James Q. (1968). *Varieties of Police Behavior*. Cambridge Massachusetts: Harvard University Press.

Worden, Robert E. (1989). Situational and attitudinal explanations of police behavior: Theoretical reappraisals and empirical assessments. *Law and Society Review* 23: 667-711.

____ (1992). The 'causes' of police brutality. Unpublished draft prepared for William A. Geller and Hans Toch, eds., *Police Use of Excessive Force and Its Control: Key Issues Facing the Nation*. Washington, DC: Police Executive Research Forum.